# BECOMING A
# CONTAGIOUS
## CHURCH

## INCREASING YOUR CHURCH'S EVANGELISTIC TEMPERATURE

Revised Edition of *Building a Contagious Church*

## MARK MITTELBERG
### FOREWORD BY BILL HYBELS

ZONDERVAN.com/
AUTHORTRACKER
follow your favorite authors

**ZONDERVAN®**

*Becoming a Contagious Church*
Copyright © 2001, 2007 by Mark Mittelberg

Requests for information should be addressed to:
Zondervan, *Grand Rapids, Michigan 49530*

**Library of Congress Cataloging-in-Publication Data**

Mittelberg, Mark.
    Becoming a contagious church : increase the evangelistic temperature in your
church / Mark Mittelberg ; foreword by Bill Hybels. — Rev. ed.
      p. cm.
    Rev. ed. of: Building a contagious church.
    Includes bibliographical references (p. ).
    ISBN-13: 978-0-310-27919-8
    ISBN-10: 0-310-27919-4
      1. Evangelistic work. 2. Church growth. I. Mittelberg, Mark. Building a contagious
church. II. Title.
    BV3790.M625 2007
    269'.2–dc22
    2007013729

*Interior design by Mark Sheeres*

*Printed in the United States of America*

07 08 09 10 11 12 13 • 10 9 8 7 6 5 4 3 2 1

*To my wife, Heidi, our daughter, Emma Jean,*
*and our son, Matthew.*
*Your love, encouragement, patience, and prayers*
*throughout this entire project*
*have meant more than words can say.*

# CONTENTS

# CONTENTS

# FOREWORD

I'VE SAID IT TIME AFTER time, but I can't help marvel once more: there's nothing like the local church when it's working right. And when churches are fully engaged in fulfilling their redemptive potential, the lost get found, the spiritually confused find truth, and lives are changed in this world and for eternity. Tell me: what other endeavor on the planet is so worthy of our time and effort?

All church leaders want to experience what it's like to be involved in an evangelistically active congregation, where every Christian is purposefully reaching out to their spiritually lost friends, neighbors, colleagues, and family members. However, the truth is that zeal for the Great Commission has grown tepid in many churches, and pastors are often uncertain about how they can lead the charge toward a new era of effective outreach.

That's where this powerful and practical book comes in. It is nothing short of a field-proven blueprint for reigniting the evangelistic fire in churches where hearts have stopped burning brightly for those outside of God's family.

This book has not been written by an academic theorist but by an active practitioner who speaks out of firsthand knowledge about evangelism in the local church. Mark Mittelberg joined our staff years ago as our first evangelism director, and he spearheaded the development of a plan to equip our entire congregation for personal evangelism. Not only has he trained thousands of people himself, but he also invented and built a whole new kind of evangelism team, creating a place of encouragement and opportunity for those with evangelistic gifts or passion throughout the entire congregation. What's more, he has innovated a number of ministries and events to seize the attention of seekers and lead them to Christ.

This book distills these developments, as well as lessons learned through interactions with other churches, into a thoroughly biblical, step-by-step process that is described through colorful stories and helpful illustrations. Frankly, I hope every church leader carefully and prayerfully studies these principles—and then summons the courage to move ahead in the power of the Holy Spirit.

After all, there's too much at stake to settle for the status quo. Lost people matter to God—and I hope you will do everything you can to apply what you learn in this book to become a contagious church that will reach them with the life-changing and eternity-altering gospel of Jesus Christ.

BILL HYBELS
Willow Creek Community Church

# INTRODUCTION

IF YOU HAVE A PASSION for reaching people with the love and truth of Christ, if you would like to develop and grow that passion, or if you care deeply about fulfilling the Great Commission and want to help your church or ministry become more effective in that endeavor—then *this book is for you!*

It doesn't matter whether your church is large or small, old or new, urban or suburban, upscale or downscale, "high church" or "low church." You may be seeker-friendly or you may not even like the term "seeker." You may be traditional, contemporary, or somewhere in between. You may be mainline, evangelical, fundamentalist, denominational, independent, conservative, progressive, or any of a hundred other labels. Perhaps you are part of a church that hates labels altogether.

You may be a pastor, a staff member, a volunteer leader, a Sunday school teacher, or a small group leader. Maybe you are a parent concerned about keeping your kids in the faith, or a church member who just cares deeply about the effectiveness of your church. What matters most is that you have a love for God, a commitment to Scripture, and a heart for the people in your community who don't yet know Christ. If that's you, read on!

This book presents biblical principles and transferable approaches for raising your church's evangelistic temperature. It offers strategies for equipping your congregation to naturally communicate their faith. It gives guidance for developing and deploying those who have latent evangelism gifts. It also presents proven ideas for initiating high-impact outreach ministries and events that will build on the diverse personalities and evangelism styles God has built into your church body.

Regardless of where you're starting from, I'm confident that with God's help you can take significant steps toward becoming a more outwardly focused and evangelistically fruitful church. In other words, *a contagious church.*

My prayer for you and your church is what the apostle Paul penned two thousand years ago in Colossians 4:5 for the earliest followers of Christ:

*Be wise in the way you act toward outsiders*

and

*make the most of every opportunity.*

Together, let's commit to doing whatever it takes in each of our communities—utilizing all of the gifts, creativity, and human resources God has provided—to reach more and more people for him.

Mark Mittelberg
Trabuco Canyon, California

# PART ONE

# A CONTAGIOUS MISSION

ORGANIZATIONS OF ALL KINDS, AND churches in particular, have a dangerous tendency to stay so busy dealing with day-to-day programs, pressures, and problems that, over time, they lose track of what they are purportedly trying to accomplish. Before they know it, they have slipped into thinking, "Mission statements, values, vision—who has time to worry about such things when we're already working overtime just trying to keep up?" But unless we step back and examine our overall direction, how can we know whether or not our efforts are taking us where we really want to go?

One thing's for sure: without intentional planning, prioritization, decision making, and leadership—and a whole lot of course corrections along the way—a church will never experience sustained evangelistic fruitfulness. This is not something churches drift into naturally or on their own. *No, becoming a contagious church only happens on purpose!* A carefully developed plan, along with supporting values and action steps, must be in place before a church can become truly effective at reaching lost people for Christ.

Building this kind of church is going to take prayer, focus, and a lot of hard work—and it's not going to happen overnight. But as we, by God's grace, begin reaching increasing numbers of friends, family members, neighbors, classmates, and coworkers, we'll know for certain that it is worth our every effort!

CHAPTER ONE

# YOUR CHURCH REACHING LOST PEOPLE

"LISTEN, I'VE TAKEN MY QUESTIONS to a pastor, a priest, and a rabbi. Not one of them was able to give me any good reasons to believe in God. In fact, they've just congratulated me for thinking it through so carefully. One of them even told me I'd given *him* some things to think about! I've spent a lot of time and energy on this, so don't think you're going to easily sway me into believing that your ideas are right."

So energized was the discussion between this young Jewish businessman and my pastor friend that a church usher actually stepped in to try to break up the "fight." But as soon as he did, both of them protested. "It's okay," my friend assured the usher, "we're both just very passionate about this."

"Not only that," added this intense seeker, "I can't tell you how refreshing it is to finally find a place like this where people seem to actually care about logic and truth. This is fantastic!" This man, like so many others today, was highly interested in discovering what is real in the spiritual realm, and he was eager to talk about it.

We see it all around us. From cover stories of national newsmagazines, to titles of bestselling books, to themes of television programs and movies, to songs on the music charts—people are hungry for information about God.

15

Spiritual interest is at a high level in our culture, but so is bewilderment about what to believe. And while there's growing suspicion of organized religion, many people, like this Jewish businessman, are still willing to turn to a church in the hope that they might—just might—find some answers.

But are we prepared to help them? Are we becoming the kind of people—and churches—that will be able to help them move forward on a spiritual journey toward Christ?

* * *

*Evangelism.* It's one of the highest values in the church—and one of the least practiced.

We all believe in it. It's on our bulletins, in our hymns, and throughout our creeds. It's posted on our marquees and peppered through our statements of faith. It's explained in our theology books, encouraged in our seminaries, and preached in our pulpits. Most Christian leaders list it as a top priority. There is little doubt that evangelism is central to what we're supposed to be about.

The irony is that while many of our churches and denominations have a rich heritage and strong reputation for evangelism, in many cases precious little is actually happening. Let's be honest: in most ministries very few people are being reached for Christ.

Yet Jesus commanded: "Go and make disciples of all nations, baptizing them in the name of the Father and of the Son and of the Holy Spirit, and teaching them to obey everything I have commanded you. And surely I am with you always, to the very end of the age" (Matthew 28:19–20). This mandate was given for all churches of all time—including yours and mine.

Since we all agree that we are supposed to be carrying out the Great Commission, why aren't we doing more about it? Studies show that most Christians don't have very many—if any—friendships with non-Christians. The majority of church members can no longer quote the words of John 3:16 about God's great love for the world, much less articulate a clear gospel illustration. A mere 14 percent of pastors claim that their churches are heavily involved in evangelism.[1]

We talk a good game, but our actions speak louder than our words. Do we really care about lost people? Are we convinced that everyone we know, without exception, needs to find the forgiveness, friendship, life, and leadership Jesus offers? Do we truly believe in hell and that our friends and family members will end up there if they don't trust in Christ before they die? Do we *really* believe that? If so, are we willing to stretch and take risks to warn them? And are we willing to invest our time and energy in developing churches that will attract, challenge, and teach them to step across the line of faith?

Jesus commissioned us to become persuasive communicators of his love and truth. That is, he asks us to become contagious Christians and to build contagious churches that will do whatever is necessary, with the guidance and power of the Holy Spirit, to bring more and more people to him. If you love Christ, I'm confident that your spirit is saying, "Yes, that's right. I long to become that kind of Christian and to be a part of that kind of church. I really want to impact people's lives and eternities!"

We were made to fulfill the Great Commission. I believe evangelism is the primary reason God left us here on the planet. We can spend all of eternity worshiping God, learning from his Word, praying, and edifying one another. But it's only here and now that we can reach lost people for Christ. We must seize the opportunity!

## THE NEED FOR CONTAGIOUS CHURCHES

What will it take to have the widespread impact we were made to have?

Relational evangelism plays a vital role. That's why I wrote *Becoming a Contagious Christian* with Bill Hybels and then developed and more recently revised and updated the *Becoming a Contagious Christian* training course and *Contagious Campaign* with Lee Strobel and Bill Hybels.[2] We wanted to equip ordinary believers to communicate their faith naturally and effectively. People come to Christ one life at a time — and usually through the influence of one or two authentic Christians who have built genuine relationships with them. All believers can and should have that kind of impact on the people around them.

But we need more than enthusiastic and equipped Christians. We also need the synergy of outwardly focused, evangelistically active churches. Churches that proactively partner with their members to reach increasing numbers of people who are far from God. Churches that are convinced that "the gates of hell shall not prevail" against them (Matthew 16:18 KJV) — and act like it. We need *contagious* churches.

I believe in the importance of these kinds of churches for two reasons. First, I've experienced how hard it is reach people outside the context of a contagious church. Second, I've experienced the benefits of doing outreach in tandem with a contagious church.

## THE LIMITATIONS OF LONE RANGER EVANGELISM

When I committed my life to Christ at age nineteen, God immediately gave me a desire to lead my friends to him. I was more than willing to talk to them about my faith. I gave them books and tapes about Christianity, led evangelistic Bible studies, organized outreach events, and, together with some friends, formed a ministry that for five years brought contemporary Christian music groups to our town to perform concerts as a way of communicating to our non-Christian friends. It was an exciting spiritual venture—though somewhat misunderstood in the rural reaches of northern North Dakota in the late '70s and early '80s!

I became known among my Christian friends for what they kiddingly referred to as "car evangelism." I would routinely invite spiritually receptive people to go for a ride so we could discuss spiritual matters or hear a tape about Christianity. We would often drive long distances along the Dakota back roads while listening to recorded gospel messages, and then talking about what we had heard. Unorthodox, perhaps. And sure, it burned up plenty of fuel. But, hey, gas was cheap back then—and many of those people made commitments to Christ and are still serving him today!

But there was a downside. This kind of outreach was isolated and independent. For many of the people I was trying to reach, I was the lone link in the spiritual chain. To the degree that a few like-minded buddies and I could sustain our efforts, we had some impact. But many times people fell through the cracks. Why? Because we were a ragtag, loosely organized team, and we weren't tightly integrated into a local church that could support or follow up on our outreach efforts.

Yes, we all were involved in various churches. But at the time, most of those churches were inwardly focused and had limited vision or energy for reaching outsiders—especially when it came to some of the newer approaches we were taking. The churches didn't know what to make of us, and we didn't know how to work with them. As a result, there was no natural handoff of seekers who wanted to go on to the next level in their search, or of new believers who needed to grow in their freshly found faith. Also, these people related to our style of communicating, but many had a difficult time connecting with the culture of the traditional churches.

At times it seemed easier to lead people to Christ than to get them into a church! Consequently, my friends and I found ourselves independently inventing solutions, piecemealing together the elements needed to keep people moving forward in their walk with Christ. We were feeling the pain of trying to be contagious Christians apart from the collaboration and support of a contagious church. God blessed many of our efforts, but the long-term results were limited compared to what could have been.

## THE POWER OF CHURCH-BASED EVANGELISM

What a difference years later when my wife, Heidi, and I moved to the Chicago area and became part of a body of believers who were learn-ing to be a contagious church! The things we had been trying to do in isolation — personal evangelism, creative outreach events, disciple-ship, Bible teaching, relevant worship, and much more — were all being done under the roof of a local church. What evangelistic power and potential!

When we built friendships with non-Christians, we now had a place to bring them to experience a church service they could relate to. When friends asked spiritual questions, we could turn to seminars, classes, teachers, recordings, and other available tools for help. When they finally made a commitment to Christ, the church had a built-in course of action for finding community, growth, and accountability in a small group.

New believers could learn to honor and exalt God in worship services that included styles of music they could relate to and teaching they could understand and apply. They could take classes to discover their spiritual gifts and take first steps toward engaging in meaningful service. They had a place to invest their time and resources to help expand God's king-dom. All of this was available at the same place that helped bring them to faith in Christ!

Heidi and I rejoiced as we watched God produce fruit in our new church. People came to Christ frequently. Testimonies of life change were common, baptisms of new believers numerous, and expectations of evangelistic impact expanding. There's a synergistic "one-two punch" when contagious Christians do relational evangelism in partnership with a contagious church that prioritizes outreach.

What about your church? It doesn't matter what brand, flavor, color, location, or age it is — there's power and potential in contagious churches everywhere that hold to the message of Christ and take risks to reach lost people.

Jesus promised, "I will build my church; and the gates of hell shall not prevail against it" (Matthew 16:18 KJV). Why are the vast majority of churches *not* growing, or growing almost exclusively through transfers of Christians from other churches? Why are so many churches losing ground, not even reaching people at the rate the population around them is growing? Why are some churches actually shutting down and closing their doors? Why are many Christians content when their church merely "holds its own" and maintains its membership and budget numbers? Could that really be what Jesus had in mind when he gave us the Great Commission? I certainly don't think so.

Bill Hybels said this to a group of church leaders:

> If you went to the airport, and there were no airplanes landing, and there were no airplanes taking off, you'd say, "There's a problem!"
> If you went to the train station, and there were no trains coming and no trains leaving, you'd say, "There's a problem!"
> So why is it that we can be a part of churches that go on year after year with almost no truly unchurched people coming to faith in Christ and with very few people really becoming more Christlike, and yet think there's no problem. Friends, if that describes your church, *"There's a problem!"*

By its very nature and purpose, the church ought to be a contagious place that is spreading the Christian faith to more and more outsiders. In fact, there ought to be an *epidemic* of people trusting in Christ. Why isn't this happening?

## CLARIFYING THE MISSION

One problem is that many churches have been around so long that they've lost sight of why they were created in the first place. Simply asking members the question, "What are we trying to do?" will often evoke blank stares or puzzled looks that seem to say, "We're not trying to *do* anything—we're a *church*, for goodness' sake!"

On the other end of the spectrum, some people will respond with an entire laundry list. "Oh, we're here to fulfill God's plan, you know, to teach people and build up the body of Christ, and to worship and grow, and train young people about God, and help needy people in the community, and to send missionaries overseas." These aren't bad goals, but they're ordered by a stream of consciousness, not by a clear sense of mission or priority. And you may have noticed that evangelism usually falls to the bottom of the list—if it's on the list at all.

Some churches try to justify their lack of activity in the area of evangelism by pointing to their other areas of strength. "We're a *teaching* church; if you want an *evangelistic* church, you should check out the one at the other end of town." Or others will say, "Sure, we believe in outreach, but *our* emphasis is praise and worship."

There is nothing wrong with churches developing strengths in particular areas. Often this is a result of God's specific calling and gifting of individual leaders and congregations. But when these strengths are developed to the *exclusion* of other basic aspects of what a biblically defined church is supposed to be like, then there's a real problem. It's like a man saying, "Sure I neglect my kids—but, hey, I'm a great husband to my wife!" Anyone can see the imbalance. Jesus gave us our universal mission statement in the Great Commission, and any church that neglects any aspect of it—including the "make disciples" part—is disregarding his divine mandate.

Churches state their evangelistic mission in different ways. Willow Creek says it's trying to "reach irreligious people and turn them into fully devoted followers of Christ." The Crossing church in Costa Mesa, California is working "to help people who are saying 'No!' to God say 'Yes!' to God in every stage and facet of their lives." Central Christian Church in Las Vegas, Nevada, wants "to connect the unconnected to Christ and together grow to full devotion to him." I went to a conference at an Episcopal church in Jacksonville, Florida. On brightly colored signs posted all over the office and classroom doors, as well as over the drinking fountain, were the words: "St. John's Cathedral: a parish congregation committed to community outreach and diocesan leadership in proclaiming the gospel of Jesus Christ." I heard about another church that has a mission statement that simply reads, "Our main thing is keeping the main thing the main thing"—and then it spells out what the "main thing" is in terms of evangelism and discipleship.

What about your church or ministry? Is your mission clear? Is it aligned with the Great Commission? Is it in the hearts of your leaders and members? Is it concise and memorable? (Leadership expert Peter

Drucker says that if you can't print your mission statement on the back of a T-shirt, it's too long!) Is it the criterion by which you make decisions about where your ministry will invest its time, energy, and money?

We must not fool ourselves. Churches will never become contagious by accident. Contagious churches result when leaders know what they're trying to build and whom they're trying to reach—and then work tirelessly in cooperation with the Holy Spirit to make it happen.

If your mission isn't clear and concise, or if it isn't clearly evangelistic, I'd urge you and your fellow leaders to draft one that is, and then begin to communicate it—*and to live by it.*

## THE SPIRITUAL CHALLENGE

Before we move on, let's address an unseen challenge: Our very real spiritual enemy, Satan, would rather keep us busy doing anything in the world other than becoming a contagious church. Satan knows all about our call to reach lost people. He understands that our mission is designed to expand God's kingdom and diminish his, so he tries to keep us tangled up in sin and selfish preoccupations. In fact, the seemingly tame sin of self-centeredness is, in my opinion, Satan's greatest weapon against evangelism.

Satan's more subtle tack is to keep us engrossed in things that are not bad, but are of lesser importance. Trivial matters. The tyranny of the urgent. The squeaky wheels. Maintenance. The good over the best. The temporal over the eternal. Anything—except reaching lost men, women, and children for Christ.

Just try to walk against the wind by becoming a contagious church, and you'll soon discover that it's a spiritual battle. True, the fight is not all with the Evil One—there are also internal struggles and sometimes conflict with people who don't understand the mission. But there is a spiritual war just the same. Ephesians 6:12 makes this very clear: "For our struggle is not against flesh and blood, but against the rulers, against the authorities, against the powers of this dark world and against the spiritual forces of evil in the heavenly realms."

Being aware of the presence and purposes of the enemy gives us a profound realization that we need to seek God daily for wisdom, guidance, strength, and protection. If we fail to pray, if we fail to fight the spiritual battle, if we don't hit our knees and enter the conflict at this level, we will miss the power and blessings of God. If we want to be contagious

Christians and to become a contagious church, prayer must be woven into the very fabric of *all* we do.

## REASONS FOR CONFIDENCE

The good news is that God really is on our side! Take to heart verses like these:

> If God is for us, who can be against us? (Romans 8:31)

> Submit yourselves, then, to God. Resist the devil, and he will flee from you. (James 4:7)

> The prayer of a righteous person is powerful and effective. (James 5:16 TNIV)

> I can do everything through him who gives me strength. (Philippians 4:13)

> I am not ashamed of the gospel, because it is the power of God for the salvation of everyone who believes. (Romans 1:16)

God will help you face problems, challenges, resistance, and misunderstandings that you encounter along the way, whether from natural or supernatural sources. I pray that he will also use what is on the pages ahead to raise your excitement and vision for what he can do through you and your church.

One of the most influential writings of our time is *Experiencing God: Knowing and Doing the Will of God* by Henry Blackaby and Claude King.[3] Its central theme is that God is always at work—he's a dynamic, active God—and our job is to find out what he's up to and join him in it. When we do that, we *know* he'll use us, because we're simply signing up for the things he is already doing!

This brings us back to where we started. Evangelism is God's idea. Jesus said his mission was "to seek and to save what was lost" (Luke 19:10). Then, before leaving, he told his followers, "As the Father has sent me, I am sending you" (John 20:21). He left us here to reach lost people—people who matter deeply to him. God assures us in his Word that he is patient with those outside his family, "not wanting anyone to perish, but everyone to come to repentance" (2 Peter 3:9). So when we partner with him we know he'll use us, because we're simply joining him in his great redemptive campaign.

Still, that's easier to say than it is to do. The obstacles are real. The odds often seem stacked against us. But let me end by telling you about a real-life church that, humanly speaking, had very little going for it.

## THE LITTLE CHURCH THAT COULD

Mount Carmel Community Church — the name sounds pretty impressive. But the church is located in Glennville, California, a desert town with an entire population of 130 people!

Here's the picture: two restaurants, one elementary school, a post office, and a church. The church was founded in 1866. When Rev. Harrell Knox joined them in the 1980s they were meeting in a small chapel building with a steeple and a bell. They had a weekly attendance of fifteen (that's fifteen *people*, not families, couples, or "giving units"). What's worse, the congregation couldn't get along with itself, and had a poor reputation due to disputes that spilled over into the community. This was hardly a candidate for becoming a highly contagious church!

Undaunted, Knox began to cast a vision for reaching unchurched people through the ministry of their little church. "Our target audience," said Knox, "is every person in a five-hundred-square-mile portion of Kern and Tulare counties — all five hundred of them!"

The members of Mount Carmel began to build relationships with the nonchurched people in their community. They knew they had to win back these people's respect and earn their trust. They started praying for these neighbors as well as for their church and its efforts to reach those who didn't know Christ.

When the leaders felt the church was ready, they launched a few outreach events. After mustering all of their talent and abilities, they found they could do four events a year — Christmas, Easter, Fourth of July, and an event at the end of Vacation Bible School in the summer. "These events are a total church effort," Knox reports. "Over 90 percent of the people serve, and more than 25 percent of the church budget is invested to make them happen!"

Being relevant to the local community called for diversity in programming and musical styles. They've used a Dixieland jazz band, a gospel rock group, a swing band, and an African-American vocal group. This wide range of music is appreciated in the region, so it is used in the outreach events along with original drama sketches, media, and a spoken biblical message.

The results? At last report, Mount Carmel had 80 to 100 people in attendance. Over 300 people from the surrounding area came to a Christmas program. And of the 500 people they are trying to reach, 350 had been touched through one or more of their programs.

On a more personal level, people like Roger, Ann, and their family have been impacted for eternity. Pastor Knox reports the following:

> Roger and Ann attended a seeker event at the urging of their daughter and others in the church who had befriended them. But then that year Rochelle became forever "sweet sixteen" in a terrible accident, and the church ministered to the family in their grief.
>
> The family began to tear apart, due in part to Roger's heart attacks and chronic alcoholism that sprang from not knowing how to deal with the grief. Krisha, the next daughter, continued to come to church and to request prayer for her daddy and the family.
>
> Miraculously God has touched their family, and Roger has prayed to receive the forgiveness and leadership of Christ. Today they are faithful members of the church, and God is using their story to bring others to himself.

## YOUR CHURCH CAN TOO

Don't you want more of that kind of fruitfulness flowing out of your life and ministry? You can! It's worth the effort, the discomfort, the risks, and the investment—it's worth it beyond what we can fully comprehend!

In the next chapter we'll begin to explore a biblical change process that will help your church grow its heart and expand its activities to reach lost people who matter so much to God—like the Jewish seeker I mentioned at the beginning, or like your son or daughter, father or mother, brother or sister, friend, neighbor, or coworker. Perhaps they've heard the truth and seen it lived out in your life but haven't yet made it their own.

Maybe, just maybe, the combined efforts of you and the other members of a contagious church—*your church*—is what the Holy Spirit will use to break through to them and help them join you in God's family, for all of eternity. You'll know it was all worth it then!

## TO CONSIDER AND DISCUSS

Becoming a contagious church that reaches unchurched people will require sustained effort and prayer. In addition, your church's leaders and members need to understand that evangelism is a central priority you're working together to accomplish.

1. Does your church have a mission statement that clearly states your intention to reach people outside of God's family? If not, that's a great place to start. If it does, is the language up-to-date? Does it speak in terms that are biblically sound but also personally compelling? Is it concise enough to be remembered?

   After making necessary adjustments (if any) to your current statement, or forming an entirely new one, write it down here:

   _____

   _____

   _____

   _____

2. Once you have a mission statement that prioritizes the value of evangelism, it must be communicated. Print it, preach on it in your worship services, and teach about it in your classes and small groups. Make it known in as many forums as possible. Jim Mellado, president of the Willow Creek Association, says, "About the time you think people are reaching communication overload, you're probably just beginning to get the message through to them!"

   The goal is to reach the point where you can ask any church member, "What is this church trying to do?" and have him or her answer reflexively, "Oh, we're trying to reach unchurched people and turn them into fully devoted followers of Christ" (or whatever your mission is). Your mission statement needs to be embedded into your culture this strongly before it will become a guiding principle in the daily decisions and actions of your church.

   What are some ways you and the church's leaders can better communicate your mission to the broader church body?

3. Make the fulfillment of your mission a matter of personal and public prayer. Ask God to work in you and in the leaders to help you become the kind of people—and your church the kind of place—that he can use to reach more and more people. Request his power, wisdom, and protection so you can defeat the schemes and attacks of the Evil One. Ask God—even right now— to help you become a truly contagious church that will reach many people for him.

# PART TWO

# CONTAGIOUS CHANGE: THE 6-STAGE PROCESS

IN PART 1 WE LOOKED at a broad snapshot of a contagious church. We saw that a contagious church is one that's clear about what it is trying to accomplish—and has evangelism squarely at the core of its mission. More than that, it views that mission not just as words on a page or a plaque, but as its God-given mandate which must be put into action in order to reach and enfold increasing numbers of people for Christ. The picture is clear. Now the stage is set for us to move toward actually *becoming* a contagious church.

But herein lies the challenge. Where to begin? What can we do to make this a driving value throughout the fabric of our church? How can we get all our members and all of our ministries to play their parts? For that matter, how do we get ourselves in the game to play our own parts?

How can we reverse the drift toward an inward focus that most churches — as well as most Christians — fall into? Short of a strong intervention, this reversal doesn't seem too likely.

So how can we intervene? What can we do to fight the gravitational pull toward self-centeredness and help our churches start becoming more and more contagious? That's what this next section is all about. In the following chapters I'll introduce the 6-Stage Process for bringing our churches, step-by-step, back to the outward focus we've discussed. Don't get me wrong: this is not an easy formula, or a simple recipe that tells you what to mix and stir — rather, it's a distillation of transferable, biblical principles that I'm confident will help you and your church, over time and with God's help, to increasingly fulfill your evangelistic mission.

Before we begin our discussion of Stage 1, let me offer a word of caution: Don't succumb to the temptation to jump immediately into launching outreach ministries and events (Stage 6). We'll get there, but we best not start there. Change must begin at a deeper level in us as the leaders and influencers of the church; as *we* change, our *church* will change. We have to start with the heart.

# CHAPTER TWO

# STAGE 1: LIVE AN EVANGELISTIC LIFE

It was a routine visit to an ordinary discount store. You know the drill. You navigate the crowded aisles surrounded by people who look as harried as you feel, but you're on your own, fending for yourself. Your goal is to find what you need, pay for it, and get out of the place — and you don't expect anyone to really notice that you were ever there.

This day, however, my experience was different. I'd barely gotten into the door of this newly built store when a woman cheerfully greeted me and offered me a shopping cart.

*That's interesting*, I thought. *I've never been welcomed like that before.*

Not much later as I was searching through the racks of merchandise, another employee walked up and asked me if I needed help finding anything. In a state of mild disbelief over actually being offered personal assistance, I reflexively replied, "No thanks, I'm just looking." After the person walked away, I came to my senses and realized that I really did need some help finding a few things, but I'd been too surprised to speak up and say what they were!

The real shocker came when I got to the checkout counter. The woman at the cash register rang up my items and, after processing my credit card and glancing at my name on the card, looked me in the eye and said, "Thank you for shopping with us today, Mr. Mittelberg."

By this point I thought I'd entered *The Twilight Zone*! In all my years of dealing with discount department stores, about the most I'd ever received from employees was vacant stares and passive indifference. I'd never encountered such friendliness, helpfulness, or courtesy. I walked out of the store that day amazed. I couldn't help wondering: "What makes this place so different?"

Whenever I've told this story in a region where one of these stores exists, the audience guesses and calls out the name of this business before I've said what it was. Perhaps you know too. Yes, it was Wal-Mart. The fact that so many people know what company I'm describing only underscores the relevancy of my question. What makes this entire chain of stores so different? Why, with few exceptions, do people who go into a Wal-Mart experience the same culture of customer service?

As I pondered this question, I was tempted to reach for simple solutions. For instance, maybe it was the result of some powerful training program for employees in which they instill respect for customers, the value of listening, and the importance of solving shoppers' problems. I was tempted to think this, but I knew the answer must go deeper.

It wasn't long after my initial visit that I began to hear more about the company's founder, Sam Walton. A peek into his beliefs and values helped me begin to understand what made this store so special.

Sam Walton was exceedingly clear about his mission — and he lived it, personally embodying the values I saw manifested in his store that day. Look at what he said about this in his autobiography, *Sam Walton, Made in America*: "Everything we've done since we started Wal-Mart has been devoted to this idea that the customer is our boss.... The customer always comes ahead of everything else."[1]

## STARTING WITH THE HEART

You and I want to help our churches become places that value and reach outsiders. How can a discussion about Sam Walton and Wal-Mart assist us in this important mission? Well, by helping us understand that the shape of an organization will be a magnification of the shape of its leaders. The mission of an organization is an extension of the mission of the leaders. The values that permeate its culture are the values of the people who run it. So if you want to reshape the priorities of any organization, you're going to have to first reshape the priorities of the men and women who guide it.

Likewise, truly contagious churches don't grow out of programs, initiatives, curricula, or trumped-up talk about "taking this town for Christ." Ultimately, they must grow out of the beliefs and values — the very *hearts* — of the people who lead them. That is why Stage 1 in the 6-Stage Process says that we must each, you and I, "LIVE an Evangelistic Life."

Wal-Mart is a customer-focused store precisely because its founder was a customer-focused leader. Your church will be an outsider-oriented ministry only if you and the other leaders become outsider-oriented leaders. It's as simple as that — and as difficult, because the hardest people in the world for any of us to change is ourselves!

Paul says in Ephesians 5:1, "Be imitators of God, therefore, as dearly loved children." He goes on to talk about loving people the way Christ did when he gave himself as a sacrifice on our behalf. In effect, Paul is saying, "Lost people matter to God; make certain they matter to you too!" This value must flow from the depths of who we are — and who we are becoming. As we've said, it really is a *heart* issue. Jesus said in Matthew 12:34: "Out of the overflow of the heart the mouth speaks." I've discovered this to be true in my own life. The condition of my heart determines the ordering of my priorities, and even the contents of my conversations.

## A HEART OVERFLOWING

Not too long ago I wanted to telephone a friend named Bill Craig. You may have heard of him; Dr. William Lane Craig is an author, lecturer, and one of the most powerful defenders of the faith today. In fact, years earlier I'd brought Bill to our church for a widely publicized debate with an atheist on the subject, "Atheism vs. Christianity: Where Does the Evidence Point?" My problem was that Bill had recently moved to a different city — and I didn't have his new phone number. So I called directory assistance and asked for the listing for William Craig; I got the number, wrote it down, and dialed it.

A cheerful voice said, "Hello!"

"Hello, I'm calling for Bill Craig," I said.

"This *is* Bill Craig," the man assured me.

"It sure doesn't sound like Bill Craig," I kidded. "I'm looking for the *real* Bill Craig."

"Well, which Bill Craig did you have in mind?" he inquired.

"I'm looking for William L. Craig," I answered.

"Well, this isn't William *L*. Craig; this is William *Z*. Craig," he said in a chipper fashion.

Now, let me interject that normally at this point I would have acknowledged I had dialed a wrong number, hung up, and left the poor guy alone. But not this day! I was walking close to Christ and living with an active awareness of the mission he gave us to "go into the world" — and I didn't want to pass up this opportunity! So I took a bit of a risk and let the more adventurous side of my personality express itself.

"That sure is too bad," I replied.

"Why's that?" he asked.

"Because you're one middle initial away from being a world-famous speaker and defender of the Christian faith!" I quipped.

"Well, you certainly do have the wrong Bill Craig," the man assured me. "No one's ever mistaken me for a *religious* person!"

"Really—why not?" I asked. "Don't you believe in God?"

"Well, yes—in my own way, I guess ..." he said, and off our discussion ran!

Now, I was as surprised by the conversation as I'm sure this stranger a thousand miles away was! But it certainly turned a routine wrong number into a meaningful discussion.

After we'd talked for a few minutes about spiritual matters I challenged him to read some of the books and materials written by his "namesake — the other, more famous Bill Craig!" Before we got off the phone, he even gave me his address, so I wrote him a letter and mailed him a recording of the debate and some other Christian publications. And all of this emanated from my punching in a wrong phone number!

That is the kind of evangelistic adventure that flows out of walking close to Christ and staying open to the split-second opportunities he often brings our way. If I had not had a Holy Spirit–boldness and a heartfelt concern for lost people that day, the conversation never would have taken place.

Unfortunately, I can illustrate the opposite situation out of my personal life, as well. When I'm spiritually disconnected and preoccupied with my own concerns and desires, I can miss even the most obvious of outreach opportunities.

## A HEART NOT FLOWING

I was on an out-of-town trip and had some time on my hands, so I decided to stop at a shopping mall to find a place to get a haircut. I remember feeling spiritually off that day. I didn't feel very close to God and, looking back, it's clear I wasn't motivated to speak to anybody about matters of faith.

The "problem" was that the woman who ended up cutting my hair was very talkative and outgoing—and she kept asking me questions about where I was from, why I was in town, what I did, and so forth. These were easy entrées into a spiritual conversation, but I'm embarrassed to admit I sidestepped them. I was immersed in my own world and preoccupied with my own concerns, and I failed to seize the chance to tell her about my ministry or my relationship with Christ. I missed a great opportunity to tell her that she is loved by God and that she can know and follow him. She was seemingly receptive; I was preoccupied and off mission.

I hate knowing that I let such an open opportunity pass me by, and tremble at the thought that God might have appointed me to help her in her spiritual journey, but I failed to speak up. (I later wrote her a note and mailed it to the salon, along with a book explaining the Christian faith, but have no idea how—or even if—it was received.) I learned a painful lesson that day: that just as it is true that "out of the overflow of the heart the mouth speaks," so also with the lack of the overflow of the heart the mouth *doesn't* speak!

## CONTAGIOUS CHRISTIANITY BEGINS WITH YOU AND WITH ME

The key for each of us as believers, and especially for Christian leaders, is to do everything we can to keep our hearts warm toward God and toward people, and then to express that warmth in ways that serve those with spiritual needs—and in the process live out this value in front of others in the church. If we want to become contagious churches, we must first become contagious Christians. The old saying really is true: "Speed of the leader, speed of the team." Jesus said it like this in Luke 6:40: "A student is not above his teacher, but everyone who is fully trained will be like his teacher." As leaders and influencers of would-be evangelistic churches, we need to be able to say with Paul, "Follow my example, as I follow the example of Christ" (1 Corinthians 11:1).

How important is our living out these values? *It's everything.* Unless you first catch God's concern for those outside his family, you may as well disregard the rest of the ideas in this book. Why? Because without a heart that beats fast for reaching people, you won't be building on the foundation needed to sustain more visible evangelistic programs and ministries.

But if we grow bigger and bigger hearts for those who don't know Christ, and if we increasingly model his bold example of being a "friend of sinners," then those around us will be inspired, and they'll take their cues from us. They too will begin taking relational risks for the sake of the gospel.

## LIVING A LIFE WORTH IMITATING

The important question is this: *how*, on a practical level, can we gain God's heart toward folks who don't know him? I'll share a few of my own ideas, but I also wanted to tap into the wisdom and experience of the wider community of outreach leaders and activists. So I wrote to many of them and asked what they do to keep their own hearts warm toward lost people. Their responses follow in the next several pages as, combined with my own thoughts, I list seven things we can do to raise our evangelism temperatures.

### 1. Admit This Value Has Slipped — And Talk to God about It

This value — evangelism — always seems to be slipping away. About the time you think you have it for good, it starts to dissipate. No one is permanently motivated to reach others for Christ. It's like water in a leaky bucket that constantly needs filling.

Think back to physics class. You may remember "the second law of thermodynamics." It tells us that everything in the physical universe, left to itself, begins slowing down, cooling off, and falling apart. This principle is evident all around us, from the crumbling of old buildings to the rust on your car's muffler to the disarray in your sock drawer. The fancy word for this is *entropy*. By the way, if you have forgotten these terms, that's just another illustration of this very principle! Our own minds move toward disorganization and entropy, so we often forget facts like these.

Similarly, there's something I've dubbed "the second law of *spiritual* dynamics." It warns us that all of us in the Christian community, left to ourselves, move away from a biblical, outward focus toward spiritual self-centeredness. The evangelism value we're trying to reinforce must constantly compete with this inward gravitational pull. The term I use for this is *evangelistic entropy*. With frightening speed, the warmest, most outreach-oriented hearts can turn into cold, inwardly absorbed hearts. The same effect can happen to entire congregations and sometimes even whole denominations.

The first step toward making a change is admitting there is a problem. Sure, we can all quote John 3:16 and talk glowingly about stories from the past, but if your passion for reaching people isn't burning brightly today, the best thing you can do is just admit it.

This is what I had to do after my visit to the hair place. I felt a low-grade guilt that I had to decide whether to run from or respond to. But why resist the Holy Spirit's whispers? We're always better off to just acknowledge the truth, let God put his finger on the problem, and respond to him accordingly.

Many of us feel guilty when it comes to evangelism. When this guilt is from God, who "disciplines those he loves" (Hebrews 12:6), it is a gift from him designed to get us back on track. But we're not supposed to wallow in the guilt. Rather, we need to let it move us toward repentance and godly action, "forgetting what is behind and straining toward what is ahead" (Philippians 3:13).

The most natural thing to do after admitting that the value of evangelism has slipped in your life is to talk to God about it. The battle to raise this value is won first in the private arena of prayer (which, by the way, was the most mentioned activity among the leaders I surveyed about the question of what they do to keep their evangelistic fervor). I like to use the classic, time-honored A-C-T-S outline. Below is an example of this prayer formula applied to evangelism. You may want to use it as a guide for your own prayer.

### A – Adoration

Father, thank you for being such a merciful and grace-filled God. I worship you for your kindness toward me and for your patience with my friends and family members who don't yet know you. Your Word says that you are slow to anger and that you don't want any of them to perish, but to come to know you. What a loving and forgiving God you are! I'm glad you are my Lord and that I have the privilege of being your child.

### C—Confession

Lord, I'm sorry I often fail to love people the way you do. You moved heaven and earth to reach them, and paid the highest price when Jesus died on the cross—yet I often resist taking even small steps to reach the people I care about. You are not willing that anyone would perish, but too often I'm afraid that I am! Please forgive and change me. Wash me of my sins of self-centeredness and fearfulness. Help me to know that as I've confessed these things, you've already been faithful to forgive and to cleanse me.

### T—Thanksgiving

Thank you that the payment Jesus made on the cross extends to me even today. I'm so glad to be in your family, to know I'm forgiven, and to have the privilege of serving you. Thank you for putting purpose in my life and for entrusting me with opportunities to make a difference in the lives of people around me. Thank you that your love and grace are examples for me as I try to express my faith to others today.

### S—Supplication

Father, help me to reflect your love toward others. Help me remember that every person I lock eyes with today matters to you. May they matter to me too—in ways that move me to action. Help me realize that if they don't yet know you, then they're lost and in desperate need of the good news of Christ. Lord, prepare me and give me boldness so I'll be able to explain your gospel well. Help me to be a genuine friend who will attract them to you and your church. Give me wisdom so I'll know how direct to be with your message, and when to back off, so I can help them keep taking steps toward you.

Please, Father, use me! Make me effective in your hands today as I try to spread your love and truth. Help me to abide in Christ and to bear much fruit. Thank you for this great privilege.

In Jesus' name, Amen.

## 2. Walk Authentically with God

Living a genuine Christian life is a prerequisite to having and expressing God's heart toward lost people. You need to be convinced through fresh, ongoing experiences with Christ, that following him is the best way to live. You must have an unwavering conviction that your friends need what you've found in him — then you will be motivated to tell them about his love.

In the *Becoming a Contagious Christian* book we talk about developing a contagious Christian character, especially in the areas of authenticity, compassion, and sacrifice. We also talk about the importance of the age-old spiritual disciplines, including prayer, Bible study, solitude, and fasting. These are the nuts and bolts of gaining the heart of God and of developing the spiritual potency needed to truly impact those around you.

Peter Grant, a former pastor and now the president of PreVision Partnerships in Atlanta, wrote, "For me there's probably nothing more motivating for evangelism than time spent in God's presence. Out of that comes a compelling desire to share the good news, not only of salvation past, but of salvation present and future as well."

"Supremely, I believe that the real incentive for witnessing comes from the worship of God," adds Robert Coleman, author of *The Master Plan of Evangelism*,[2] in his response to my question. Coleman is a man who has modeled God's heart for lost people for over half a century. "It is the adoring love of Christ," he went on to observe, "that compels us to declare the glory of his grace."

In keeping with this, an authentic life of walking with God starts with and flows out of personal spiritual alignment. Notice the progression in Psalm 51, verses 9–12, when King David admits and repents of his sins:

> Hide your face from my sins
> and blot out all my iniquity.
> Create in me a pure heart, O God,
> and renew a steadfast spirit within me.
> Do not cast me from your presence
> or take your Holy Spirit from me.
> Restore to me the joy of your salvation
> and grant me a willing spirit, to sustain me.

Then, after addressing his own condition before God, David's very next thought, in verse 13, is to proclaim God's grace to others:

> Then I will teach transgressors your ways,
> and sinners will turn back to you.

Similarly, John 15:5 tells us that if we'll abide in Christ and let him abide in us, we'll bear much fruit.

"I hang out with God every day," noted Becky Pippert, an inspiring evangelistic example, and author of the classic book, *Out of the Saltshaker and Into the World*.[3] "How can we engage in intimate dialogue with God and not become aware of his heart? The apostle Paul tells us in 2 Corinthians 3:18 that simply by gazing into the face of Christ we become transformed into his likeness. That means that the more time we spend in God's presence, the more we have something to say and give to others."

In addition, God loves to answer the prayers of his authentic followers for increased evangelistic opportunities. Joe Aldrich, longtime evangelism activist and author of the groundbreaking book, *Lifestyle Evangelism*,[4] wrote this to me in a letter: "I have had dry spells in my 'efforts in evangelism.' On several occasions I have prayed that the Lord would bring a prepared heart across my path, and sometimes within twenty-four hours that is exactly what happened. That is always a joy and confirmation!"

### 3. Spend Time in Select Passages of Scripture

Bill Hybels often talks about how he was influenced early in his ministry by the message of Luke 15 — where Jesus, in response to the religious leaders' calloused attitudes toward spiritual outsiders, told three stories in rapid succession that illustrated how much lost people matter to the Father. Bill's life and ministry were marked by the lessons of the lost coin, the lost sheep, and the lost son — and the heart of God that is revealed through them. This deeply impacted the shape and priorities of the church Bill started, and of thousands of other churches he continues to influence around the world.

I find myself especially motivated when I review John 4 and see how Jesus interacted with the woman at the well. He showed concern for somebody society had written off. He winsomely piqued her curiosity by talking about "spiritual water" in order to start a spiritual conversation. He forthrightly told her he was the Messiah. Then he allowed her time to go get her friends and bring them back to the well to hear more about his message and mission.

What impresses me most in this passage is how, after spending time with this social outcast, Jesus summed up his experience by telling the disciples, "I have food to eat that you know nothing about.... My food ... is to do the will of him who sent me and to finish his work" (John 4:32, 34). In effect he was saying, "I don't care who this person is, what she has done, or where she stands on the social ladder. I just had a chance to alter the eternity of a human being who matters more to my Father than any of you can imagine—*and I eat that up!*"

The reason Jesus' words affect me so much is that I've experienced what it feels like to be so caught up in the exhilaration of sharing Christ with another person that I really don't care about eating or sleeping or any other seemingly trivial physical matters. On the other hand, I've known all too often what it's like to be consumed by daily concerns and distractions and to lose focus on my primary purpose. So when I read Jesus saying, "My food is to do the will of him who sent me," my spirit says, *"Yes! That's what I want to experience a lot more of the time."* It raises the value of evangelism in me and warms my heart toward people who need God.

Perhaps other passages will impact you in similar ways: maybe John 3, Jesus' encounter with Nicodemus; or Luke 19, the story of Jesus and Zacchaeus; or Acts 1–2, Peter and the spread of the gospel in Jerusalem; or Acts 8, Philip and the Ethiopian; or Acts 26, Paul boldly taking a stand for the gospel and evangelizing some of the very people who put him on trial for his faith! Or, like me, maybe Luke 16 and the story of the rich man and Lazarus moves you, with its clear warnings about the reality of heaven and hell—and how our eternal destiny is sealed at death. This is a sobering reminder of the importance and urgency of reaching out to tell others now about God's salvation.

The list of Bible passages could go on and on. What's important is that you find one or two (or three or four) that make your evangelistic heart beat quickly. Then meditate on them, write them out, post them where you'll see them often. Teach on them when you have opportunity. Maybe memorize some of them too, and let God's vision fill your heart and move you to action.

## 4. Review What God Has Done in Your Life

Dr. James Martin, pastor of Mount Olivet Baptist Church in Portland, Oregon, told me, "Because I know what I was and what Christ has done for me, I want others to know God's love and to experience the freedom and peace I have in Christ even in the midst of a troubled world."

Similarly, Christian leader and author Chuck Colson said to me in a letter:

> What happened in Tom Phillips's driveway years ago when I surrendered my life to Christ remains as vivid in my memory and consciousness today as it was at the time. I have never forgotten—and I don't want to forget—what happened that night. I realized for the first time in my life that I was a sinner, desperately in need of salvation and forgiveness. And that night it became clear to me that God was offering that to me—that Jesus Christ the Son of God actually went to the cross, died in my place, and took my sins upon himself, enabling me to be free.
>
> Now, if someone does that for you, how do you respond? G. K. Chesterton said that gratitude is the mother of all virtues. One should be overwhelmed with gratitude for what God has done for us, and this gratitude then inspires us to do our duty, to do whatever God calls us to do. And the simple fact is that Jesus calls us to share that good news.

Over and over I've seen that when we review God's merciful activity in our own lives, our passion grows for spreading his mercy to others. Reflect on the story of how God reached you, and you'll find yourself becoming more motivated to tell others of his love and salvation.

## 5. Spend Time with Other Contagious Christians

One of the most important ways I keep my evangelistic fervor is by spending time with others who live out this value in their own lives. This is especially true of the time I spend with my close friend and ministry partner, Lee Strobel. He and I have done ministry together for many years. One of our favorite things is going out for lunch somewhere with no formal agenda and just letting our imaginations and conversations run free with ideas of things we could try in order to reach people for Christ. (Many of the ministries and events I talk about in this book have come out of these times together.) As Hebrews 10:24 puts it, we "spur one another on toward love and good deeds"—and nowhere is this more important than evangelism!

And what's exciting is that this kind of influence usually goes both ways. Here's an email I got from another church leader I had recently spent time with and was encouraged by. It illustrates the effect Christians can have on one another when we spend time together dreaming about reaching folks for Christ:

> Thanks again, Mark, for the burst of encouragement you have
> provided me—especially personally. I simply cannot express the
> wonderful feeling of being with brothers of like mind with regard
> to lost people. This is especially so in light of the spiritual desert
> I've felt I have been traveling alone in for so long. It's nice to have
> the wind at your back once in a while!

Who could you get a "burst of encouragement" from? It might be someone in your church, a leader from another church in your area, or someone from the other side of the country—but whoever it is, find ways to stay in touch with them. Invest in the relationship. Pray together, challenge one another, and watch God work!

Let me add that while you certainly can't have lunch with Dwight L. Moody, you can "spend time" with him by reading books such as *A Passion for Souls*[5] by Lyle Dorsett and experience a similar effect. I doubt that it's possible to read about the life of Moody and *not* have your own passion for souls charged up. The same is true when you read about Salvation Army founders William and Catherine Booth, John Wesley, Hudson Taylor, William Carey, and many others.

Most of us will never have personal access to someone like Billy Graham, but we can listen to his messages and read his autobiography, *Just As I Am*.[6] When we do, some of his contagious influence rubs off on us. Rick Warren can have a similar effect through *The Purpose Driven® Church*,[7] as can Bill Bright, through reading the powerful biography of his life, *Amazing Faith*,[8] and his world-impacting ministry with Campus Crusade for Christ.

Even at a distance, people such as Chuck Colson, Luis Palau, Ravi Zacharias, Greg Laurie, and Bill Hybels can impact our attitudes and help us become more driven to reach the seekers who live all around us.

So get around the right people, as well as the influence of people you can't get around, and let their evangelistic hearts affect yours. It will help you to live out this vital value in powerful ways.

## 6. Get in the Game

Other than the emphasis on prayer, the most common response I received to my question on how we can keep our evangelistic embers burning brightly was that we need to simply get out of the lab and spend time with real non-Christians. After decades of teaching others to do evangelism, D. James Kennedy told me he continues "the discipline of going out weekly with our *Evangelism Explosion* teams, which keeps the edge on your evangelistic sword."

Wayne Cordeiro, a man who stays extremely busy as the pastor of the burgeoning New Hope Christian Fellowship O'ahu in Honolulu, Hawaii, told me one of the main ways he keeps motivated is to "take time to be with people. I play on a city league soccer team every Tuesday evening, I belong to the Rotary Club, and I often speak to companies about leadership, excellence, and restructuring. This keeps me in contact with non-Christians weekly."

Two of my own spiritual mentors, the now-deceased Bob Passantino and his wife, Gretchen, wrote, "We think one of the big mistakes Christian leaders make is that they tell their listeners to witness to the unsaved, but they themselves spend all their time in a Christian cocoon and don't regularly do what they teach others to do. There are lots of ideas that sound good, but until you experience their practical application, you can't effectively equip others to do the same."

Gene Appel, lead pastor of Willow Creek Community Church, said "Nothing keeps my embers for the lost 'hot' like sharing my faith. The more I get to interact with lost people the more fired up I become. The more distant I get, the colder my heart gets."

Actual face-to-face interaction with people who don't know Christ is, without question, what motivates me more than anything else. I can listen to good teaching about evangelism, read Scripture verses about the priority of spreading the good news, and hear statistics about how many new unchurched families are moving into the neighborhoods around the church, but nothing moves me like getting to know a few real people who need God. Then they are no longer nondescript, generic "seekers." They are people I care about, with real names and faces. And I'll do whatever I can to try to help them meet Christ. How can you *not* value lost people when they've become your close friends?

The challenge, especially if you've been a Christian for a long time, is to deliberately step out of your comfort zone and get yourself around some people who matter to God, but to whom God may not yet matter. They're going to talk differently—and sometimes much more "colorfully"—than you and your church friends, value things you don't value, take part in things you don't like or agree with, and at times make you feel uncomfortable. But before you get discouraged, just think about how the sinless Son of God must have felt when he came to this sin-tainted planet and walked among us, "seeking and saving that which was lost." Let his love and example—and the fruit of his efforts—inspire you to do what he did. It'll be a stretch at first, but before long you'll see that it's the adventure of your life! And sooner or later some of those wayward friends are going to come back around and thank you for doing what it took to reach them with the love of the Savior.

## 7. Follow God's Promptings

The final thing I'll mention that will help us live out evangelism values is listening to God's voice and staying attuned to his leadings. Chuck Colson wrote this to me:

> I have disciplined myself to listen to the Holy Spirit. For example, I was giving the closing lecture at the C. S. Lewis Conference in Oxbridge recently, and in the prayer time ahead of my speech, one of my colleagues prayed for those who might be there from the Cambridge campus who were spiritually adrift or searching or seeking. Halfway through my talk when I was describing the influence of Lewis on my life, I stopped and said, "I'd like to share the same message with you that Lewis shared with me." We had a prayer of invitation in the middle of the closing address at the Oxbridge Conference! But that's only because I felt the prompting of the Spirit.

Lee Strobel relayed a similar experience that happened at a more personal level. He was meeting people after he had spoken at one of the outreach services at Willow Creek. A man poured out his heart to Lee about issues he was facing and told him how much he needed God's help. Lee said his natural inclination was to simply encourage the man a bit and offer to pray for him. But Lee was dialed in to the voice of the Spirit, who prompted him instead to challenge the man concerning what was keeping him from trusting Christ. Before their time together was over, the man prayed with Lee to receive Jesus as his forgiver and leader.

Who knows what exciting doors of spiritual influence God will take us through if we will just listen to his voice and do what he tells us. God is actively reaching out to lost people. We just need to respond to his promptings and seize the opportunities he provides. When we do, he'll use us to touch the hearts of others—and in the process he'll work in us, too, expanding our own hearts.

## LIVING EVANGELISTIC VALUES

How about you? Are you so busy with church work that you don't have time to do the most important work of the church? Especially as Christian leaders, we have to set aside needless meetings, unessential appointments, and the ever-present sense of busyness, and make certain we are getting up close to the people God wants to reach.

Let the love of God and your love for people motivate you. And let others in the church see what you're doing. Let them watch you build relationships with nonbelievers. Talk to them about your efforts to start spiritual conversations and convey biblical truths to your friends. Tell them when it goes well, and tell them when it doesn't. They'll learn from your successes and your failures—and will be inspired by both.

I know from my years at Willow Creek that a primary reason it is such an evangelistic church is because its founding pastor, Bill Hybels, consistently lives out this value. You may have read in the opening pages of the *Becoming a Contagious Christian* book about Bill's decision to participate in sailboat racing with a completely non-Christian crew—and then later in the book's closing pages how Tommy, one of the toughest guys on that crew, gave his life to Christ. I was at the church several years later when Bill informed the congregation that the fourth person from his racing team circle made a commitment to Christ after one of our holiday outreach services. Then, during that summer's baptism service we all watched Bill baptize Dave out in the church pond. These changes in the lives of his friends obviously keeps Bill motivated, but it also inspires the rest of the church.

## ENJOYING THE ADVENTURE: RISKS, REWARDS, AND ALL

If you think about it, Bill's decision to put together a sailing crew of non-Christians was a pretty risky move. What about the bad influence they may have had on him? What about the negative impact they could have had on his reputation as a Christian leader?

I've discovered that no matter who you are, what role you play in the church, or what step God is leading you to take in evangelism, big or small, it will always feel to some degree risky. It might be a relationship to build, a conversation to start, a question to ask, a misconception to correct, a group to train, an event to initiate, or any number of other possibilities. Whatever it is, it's going to feel a bit threatening, and you're going to be tempted to put it off or skip it entirely. Perhaps you've been avoiding it for some time already?

Both the Old and New Testaments tell us "the righteous will live by faith" (Habakkuk 2:4; Romans 1:17). The Christian life involves living in dependence on God. That was true in a major way when we trusted God for salvation, but the Bible is saying much more than that. Notice the verses do not merely say, "The righteous initially received eternal life by faith." Rather, they say we *live*—present tense—by faith.

Just what is faith? One way to view it is as "God-directed risk": living based on simple trust in God's promises and unseen protection, obeying his unseen Spirit, building his unseen kingdom, looking forward to his as-of-yet unseen home in heaven. It's the risk of taking him at his word and finding him completely trustworthy. A rough paraphrase of the verse might be, "The righteous will live lives marked by patterns of obedient, God-honoring risk-taking." The question is this: Are you living by that kind of biblical faith?

To at least some degree we must be *courageous* Christians if we're to become *contagious* ones. We must get on board with what Scripture and God's Spirit are leading us to do, even if it is new, even if it seems unusual, even if it might be misunderstood. We have to move ahead and set the pattern for the rest of the church. We need to lead the way and then, like the apostle Paul, say to the others, "Follow my example, as I follow the example of Christ" (1 Corinthians 11:1). We must show what it looks like to live out the value that lost people matter to the Father and also to us. If we'll do this, soon they'll matter a whole lot more to our churches too, and we'll be well on our way toward creating and sustaining a genuine evangelistic culture—the kind that cares for lost people in even greater ways than Wal-Mart cares for its customers.

Contagious churches grow out of the flaming hearts of contagious leaders and contagious Christians. But as we'll see in the next chapter, you'll need to take intentional steps to spread what's in your heart into the hearts of those around you.

## STAGE 1: KEY IDEA

*The first step toward becoming a contagious church is living a contagious life.*

Set an example for the believers in speech, in life, in love, in faith and in purity. (1 Timothy 4:12)

# TO CONSIDER AND DISCUSS

1. What pours gasoline on the evangelistic fire in your heart? What do you need to do to pour on a gallon or two today?

2. Are you investing time praying for those outside of God's family? Do you need to adjust your schedule to make more time for prayer? Why not take a few moments right now to pray for the people in your life who need to know Christ?

3. Is there an area in which God has been prompting you to act or speak but you have been resisting?

4. Is there a divine prompting you have responded to recently? How did God work through your efforts?

5. What practical steps do you need to take to immerse yourself in passages of God's Word that will ignite your heart for evangelism?

6. What non-Christian friend or family member will you commit to spending time with in the next week or two? What will you do together?

# CHAPTER THREE

# STAGE 2: INSTILL EVANGELISTIC VALUES IN THE PEOPLE AROUND YOU

I WAS MEETING WITH SEVERAL high-level ministry leaders who wanted input on how they could increase the value and priority of evangelism among their leadership peers. "We do a pretty good job of nurturing new believers and growing up those who are already followers of Christ," one said, "but we're weak in outreach. We want to help our ministry become more effective at reaching people with the gospel. Where do you think we should start?" It was a great question.

These leaders already lived evangelistic lives in many of the ways we discussed in chapter two. They did not lack a commitment or passion for evangelism. But the ministry they led was a different story. It was filled with warmhearted believers who mainly focused their ministry efforts on the already convinced.

In his book *The Purpose Driven® Church*, Rick Warren tells of a survey done by Win Arn, a leading church consultant:

> He surveyed members of nearly a thousand churches asking the question, "Why does the church exist?" The results? Of the church members surveyed, 89 percent said, "The church's purpose is to take care of my family's and my needs." For many, the role of the pastor is simply to keep the sheep who are already in the "pen"

happy and not lose too many of them. Only 11 percent said, "The purpose of the church is to win the world for Jesus Christ."[1]

Then the *pastors* of the same churches were asked the same question. Amazingly, the results were exactly the opposite. Of the pastors surveyed, 90 percent said the purpose of the church was to win the world, and 10 percent said it was to care for the needs of the members. Is it any wonder we have conflict, confusion, and stagnation in many churches today?

In spite of the good intentions of their leaders, somewhere along the way most of the ministries they lead start turning inward. They begin investing more and more of their time, energy, and resources in plans that serve insiders. They don't think very much about how they can reach people for Christ but, rather, whether the church is doing all it should to meet their own needs and expectations.

Now, many of those needs are in line with the broader purposes of the church and, therefore, important. But when the mission of the church gets reduced to keeping the sheep in the pen happy, the mission is falling woefully short. I'm sure the ninety-nine sheep in Jesus' parable believed they deserved the undivided attention and protection of their shepherd. I can even imagine several of them complaining, "What's the big deal about finding one little lost sheep when there are so many of us right here who need a good meal and a safe place to sleep?"

Clearly in Jesus' mind finding the lost sheep was—and still is—a big deal. Therefore, we have to work to overcome this tendency toward self-absorption and regain an outward focus.

## ATTACK ON EVERY FRONT

"This may not be what you want to hear," I said to my ministry leader friends, "but in my opinion, you're going to have to declare an all-out war! If you want to change values and create a real evangelistic culture, you're going to have to attack on every front—and do so relentlessly. You can't let up until your team has adopted a whole new set of priorities and is living them out day to day."

Why was I so bold about this? It's not because I'm a person who enjoys warfare! I had three reasons: First, because *God has given us nonnegotiable marching orders.* Jesus was clear about his own mission: He came "to seek and to save what was lost" (Luke 19:10). Then later he made it clear that he was sending us into the world to further this mission

(John 17:18). And, lest there be any confusion, he summarized our task one more time when he said in Matthew 28:19, "Therefore go and make disciples of all nations."

There is no ambiguity about our mission. We just need to keep it clear in our own hearts and minds and then do all we can to get it into the hearts and minds of those around us. Pastor Gene Appel said it to me like this: "When the church is absolutely clear on what the 'main thing' is, it makes you face it at every turn—in the way you pray, plan, prepare, preach, and give." This is true not just of the leaders but of everyone in the body who understands and supports the "main thing."

My second reason: *we really are in a war!* I know this is strong language that conjures up images of conflict, weapons, and life-and-death struggle. But this is the kind of battle we're actually fighting. Look at what Paul wrote in 2 Corinthians 10:3–5:

> For though we live in the world, we do not wage war as the world does. The weapons we fight with are not the weapons of the world. On the contrary, they have divine power to demolish strongholds. We demolish arguments and every pretension that sets itself up against the knowledge of God, and we take captive every thought to make it obedient to Christ.

And as we mentioned in chapter one, Paul also wrote in Ephesians 6:12–13:

> For our struggle is not against flesh and blood, but against the rulers, against the authorities, against the powers of this dark world and against the spiritual forces of evil in the heavenly realms. Therefore put on the full armor of God, so that when the day of evil comes, you may be able to stand your ground.

In our battle for the souls of men and women, we have an enemy who is giving it all he's got to try to sidetrack or stop us. It's going to take relentless effort and the power of the Holy Spirit to prevail in our mission and mobilize our members to the cause.

Third, *I know, from my own ministry of helping churches with evangelism, how difficult it is to turn the ship around and get real ownership of the mission.* One of the greatest leadership challenges you'll ever face is trying to convince people to follow your example and look beyond their own needs to the "main thing" of valuing and reaching those outside God's family.

## OUR BUSINESS EXAMPLE

Think back to the example of Wal-Mart. Its founder, Sam Walton, personally modeled great customer service, but he also went the next step and worked hard to instill this value into the people who worked with him. In his autobiography, *Sam Walton, Made in America*, we get a glimpse of his tenacious commitment to communicate this value: "For my whole career in retail, I have stuck by one guiding principle. It's a simple one, and I have repeated it over and over and over in this book until you're sick to death of it. But I'm going to say it again anyway: the secret of successful retailing is to give your customers what they want."[2]

What can we take away from this? We must have that kind of commitment and passion for instilling into our church members the biblical principle of giving people not necessarily what they want, but what they really need — the love and truth that are found only in Jesus Christ!

In a later section of his book, under the heading "Communicate, Communicate, Communicate," Walton adds emphatically, "The necessity for good communication in a big company like this is so vital it can't be overstated."[3] Remember how on my first experience at a Wal-Mart I was surprised by the store's extraordinary level of service, including the attention of a friendly employee who walked over to see if I needed any help? Well, near the time when that store opened, Walton reports that he sat in front of a camera and broadcast a message by satellite link to Wal-Mart employees all over the country. He said to them:

> I want you to take a pledge with me. I want you to promise that whenever you come within ten feet of a customer, you will look him in the eye, greet him, and ask him if you can help him....
>
> Now, I want you to raise your right hand — and remember what we say at Wal-Mart, that a promise we make is a promise we keep — and I want you to repeat after me: From this day forward, I solemnly promise and declare that every time a customer comes within ten feet of me, I will smile, look him in the eye, and greet him.[4]

Wow! You get the impression he was serious, don't you? It's no wonder he was able to build such a customer-oriented organization — and that I saw such a clear manifestation of his influence that day I first visited one of his stores.

## THE CHALLENGE FOR US

Leaders who communicate a value as consistently and aggressively as Sam Walton did will reshape, over time, the culture of their entire organization. The same can be true for us in our efforts to spread evangelistic values in our church.

Again, we need to start, as we discussed in chapter two, with Stage 1 of our 6-Stage Process, as we "LIVE an Evangelistic Life." There's an adage that says, "You can't give away what you don't already have." Applied here, it means the evangelism mission must take root first in our own hearts and lives.

But many well-meaning leaders stop there. They fail to communicate this vision to the key influencers around them. They work in isolation, holding their dream of widespread evangelistic impact close to their chest. They don't realize that without broad ownership of outreach-oriented values, these efforts will almost certainly fail. That's why we can't ignore Stage 2 in the 6-Stage Process, which is to "INSTILL Evangelistic Values in the People around You." This step is critical because, as Joe Aldrich wrote to me, "In my estimation, the number-one challenge in churches is to get the leadership to not only model an outward focus, but to make it a matter of lifestyle in the congregation."

How can we do this? Here are some ideas to help you get started.

## INSTILLING EVANGELISTIC VALUES

### Pray for It

It seems ingrained in some of our personalities that we should work hard first—and then pray only if we get stuck! But even Jesus, the very Son of God, prayed hard first—and then he worked. We need to follow his example.

We need to also challenge everyone we lead to pray for lost friends and family members. In the updated *Becoming a Contagious Christian* evangelism course, we encourage every participant to keep an "Impact List" of three names of people in their sphere of influence whom they want to see come to know Christ. We teach them to pray regularly for these people and then to take steps to deepen those relationships and to initiate spiritual conversations. This has proven to be a great way to instill the value of evangelistic prayer and activity.

We should also encourage outreach-related prayer times at the various meetings, classes, and services that take place throughout the church. We occasionally do this in our churchwide worship services. We hand out cards on which people can write their friends' names. Then we ask them to pair up and take turns praying for their friends. This is a great way to raise evangelistic awareness and inspire commitment among members. It also gets them involved all at once in taking a tangible step—praying—to reach people for Christ.

Another idea is to have a short prayer time at the end of your Communion services. In addition to thanking God for the sacrifice Jesus made on the cross, give members a moment to pray for one unchurched friend or family member they would like to have sitting next to them as a new brother or sister in Christ at a Communion service in the future. This will bring a whole new appreciation to the meaning and application of Christ's redemptive work.

Unless the Holy Spirit is working in and through us, nothing of lasting value is going to happen. So we must ask God to increasingly energize this value in our own hearts, as well as in the hearts of the people in our church or ministry.

## Lead It

The leaders of your church need to make it clear that evangelism is central to what your ministry will be about, and that there is no room for debate on this. Why? Because our ultimate Leader, Jesus, has already prescribed it.

I heard a pastor in Dallas, Texas, present the priority of evangelism to his church in a compelling vision message. He said:

> You know, we love to vote on things. We vote on everything! But not on this one thing—because this one is not up to us to decide. Jesus already told us what our mission is. When he said, "Go into all the world and make disciples," he didn't leave room for deliberation or debate. We just need to see his vision for the church, make that vision ours, and spend our energy finding ways to implement it as quickly and effectively as we possibly can!

In his book *Doing Church as a Team*, pastor Wayne Cordeiro said, "There's one thing worse than a church without vision. It's a church with many visions! In this kind of congregation, everyone is lobbying for their own personal agendas and the church ends up becoming a political body of individuals, each one pulling for his or her own viewpoint. With too many visions, a church will have the seeds of dissension at its very inception."[5]

People need to know where the church is going. They need to know that Christ's evangelistic mission is your mission — and top priority. So say it again and again in whatever circles of influence you have as a leader or influencer. If you want people to become personally and sacrificially involved, then convince them that your mission is biblical, Christ-honoring, essential, and urgent — and the eternities of the people around them depend on it.

It's often said in corporate circles that the vision of any business must be restated every twenty-eight days or else workers lose sight of their purpose and revert to older, less productive patterns. What's true in industry, at least in this area, is true for us in the church. If we're to overcome the second law of spiritual dynamics — evangelistic entropy — it's going to take a constant lifting of people's vision in order to overcome the gravitational pull toward self-centeredness.

We all have roles to play in this effort, but the senior pastor in particular needs to lift the church's vision in small ways regularly and in big ways annually or semiannually. Many churches have an annual "Vision Night," where the pastor teaches again about the church's mission, values, and strategy, and then challenges every member to commit to doing his or her part in executing that plan. When evangelism is central to that vision, this will go a long way toward instilling it as a value in the entire congregation.

## Tell the Truth about It

A vital part of leadership is honest communication about the problem you hope to overcome. But this can feel threatening, so many leaders are tempted to hide or soften the truth. But caving in to this temptation is shortsighted and will prevent you from making the changes necessary to really win.

So if you've only had one genuine adult conversion through the ministry of your church in the last year, say so. If thirty-six out of thirty-nine recent baptisms involved church transfers or children of church families, admit this to be the case. If you have a membership of 1,200 but only 400 people actively attend services each week, don't hide behind the 1,200 figure. If nine out of ten people who "make decisions" during altar calls are merely deciding to transfer membership from another church, don't pretend that revival is breaking out. If only a small percentage of the people in the neighborhoods around your church actually attend a church, let your members know about the problem. If that percentage has dropped three points since the previous poll, talk about it as a matter of real concern and prayer—and then appropriate action. If feedback from nonchurched visitors says that your church is unfriendly, or hard to relate to, or "stuck in the '70s," then make it a topic of constructive discussion.

In his must-read book, *Leading Change*, Harvard professor John Kotter says that the first step in bringing about change is to magnify the problem. "Establishing a sense of urgency," Kotter says, "is crucial to gaining needed cooperation. With complacency high, transformations usually go nowhere because few people are interested in working on the change problem." Later he adds, "People will find a thousand ingenious ways to withhold cooperation from a process that they sincerely think is unnecessary."[6]

The way we convince people that change is necessary is by breaking the bad news of how far we're falling short of fulfilling our mission. This news can be delivered in the form of numbers or stories—preferably both. But bad news becomes the vehicle for eventual good news if it wakes people up and causes them to take decisive action. Truly, the only thing worse than the pain of change is the pain of staying the same when change is what is really needed.

Can you see why we started in Stage 1 at the heart-and-values level? If lost people really matter to us, then we have no choice but to move to Stage 2 and try to spread these values throughout the church. We must speak the truth, admit where we're missing the mark, and cultivate hearts that are willing to make the necessary changes.

## Teach It

Whether you are the pastor, a small group leader, a Sunday school teacher, or the head of one of the ministries of the church, you have a vital role. One of the most important ways you can raise the evangelism temperature in your church is through the straightforward teaching of these biblical values.

Teach regularly from some of the key passages we discussed earlier—Luke 15, John 4, or Acts 1–2. Remember that the evangelism value, more than any other, needs to be lifted over and over. Keep reinforcing it by showing the actions of leaders in the Bible, especially Jesus.

If you're a pastor, it's important to preach a Sunday series about evangelism on a regular basis. This is one of the most effective ways to help people in your church gain this value and see that evangelistic activity should be a normal part of the Christian life. You can build this kind of series around some of the passages we've mentioned or use the six *Contagious Campaign* message transcripts from Bill Hybels, Lee Strobel, and me (adapt them as necessary) that come with the updated *Becoming a Contagious Christian* curriculum,[7] which we'll discuss in greater detail in chapter five. In addition, there are four messages in Bill Hybels' series, *Just Walk Across the Room.*[8] These tools are designed to make it easier to teach this important value and instill it in the hearts and habits of the people in your church (many churches use one of these series during one season, and the other during the next).

Also, help your members understand that what you are teaching is not some recent idea. It's rooted in the original mission of your church's founders (virtually every church was planted with the initial desire and vision to reach people in a new part of town or more distant region). Help them see that any changes needed to become more evangelistic are not really about something new, but something very old — the clear mandate of Scripture and the strong vision of your own spiritual forebears.

From time to time you may also need to address the issue of separatism. Some members may have grown up in settings where leaders took Bible verses out of context to make it appear that we are to resist contact with non-Christians — that they're the enemy to be avoided at all costs. If any traces of this exist in your congregation, you need to go after it with passion. I wrote about this problem in the updated *Becoming a Contagious Christian Leader's Guide*:

> First, God does warn us to use caution, because the dangers are real. Jesus said, "I am sending you out like sheep among wolves" (Matthew 10:16a) — a dangerous idea from its very inception! That's why he immediately adds that we need to be "as shrewd as snakes and as innocent as doves" (Matthew 10:16b). But note that Jesus is the one sending us out there — this was *his* idea.
>
> Second, a closer look at the verses that talk about being separate reveals that they are referring primarily to separation from the *sins* of people, not necessarily the people themselves. Jesus prayed that we would be in the world, but not of the world (John 17:15). Jesus was the best model of this. We should follow his example and be

friends with people in the world, without being a friend to or in any way compromising with the evil in the world.

Finally, in any relationship with a nonbeliever, we must remain the dominant moral and spiritual influence. Otherwise the person becomes to us the kind of bad influence the Bible warns about (1 Corinthians 15:33). It is then necessary to pull back, at least for a season, and do whatever is necessary to reestablish our spiritual strength and influence.[9]

When it comes to instilling the value of evangelism, don't underestimate the importance of clear, passionate biblical teaching — you can't become a contagious church without it.

An important note about "Teach It": Teachers can't rely purely on message series to raise evangelism values. Why? Because you must cycle through a variety of topics and Scripture passages to serve up a balanced diet to the church. Yet this value needs to be lifted constantly. So what can you do?

Elevate the value of evangelism through illustrations, even when you're teaching about something completely different. I heard a pastor preach about the Holy Spirit, but he didn't just talk about the guidance, gifts, and nature of the Holy Spirit. He also emphasized the *influence* of the Holy Spirit, seen throughout the book of Acts as people who were filled with the Spirit testified boldly about Jesus Christ. His listeners learned about the third person of the Trinity generally, but they were especially made aware of the Holy Spirit's desire to help us tell others about Jesus.

I heard another pastor preach about how we can discern God's will for our lives. One of his key illustrations was about a recent experience he'd had in which the Spirit led him to share God's love with someone who was sitting alone outside a store. The main subject of his message was *guidance*, but a key value being reinforced was *evangelism*.

Keep this value in front of the people to whom you speak whenever you can, regardless of what your primary topic is at the moment.

## Study and Discuss It

Another thing we can do is encourage members to discuss evangelism in small groups. Doing so will help them process and adopt evangelistic values. Studying key outreach-oriented Bible passages will be helpful, as will reading books like *Inside the Mind of Unchurched Harry and Mary, How to Give Away Your Faith*, and *Out of the Saltshaker and Into the*

*World.* Also, the updated *Becoming a Contagious Christian* curriculum is now designed to be taught in small groups using a new "plug-and-play" teaching DVD. All of these approaches are especially effective when done in concert with vision and teaching from the pulpit. Remember, we're declaring war—and attacking on every front!

## Disciple It

If we're serious about instilling the value of evangelism into the people around us, we need to make it a central theme as we disciple others. Occasionally that may include direct but loving challenges to church members who are refusing to let God's heart for lost people affect them. But more often it will be gentle reminders about this value and respectful questions about their progress with people they are trying to reach.

I'm not suggesting heavy-handed, controlling kinds of discipleship. I'm talking about personal communication with a few key people who want coaching to help them become more like Christ. I'm also talking about two-way accountability, where your colleagues have the freedom to ask you the same questions you're asking them. Another important aspect is actually partnering with these people by getting to know some of their friends and family, and trying to help them communicate their faith to those folks. Jesus modeled this by sharing his life with his disciples for three years. Paul stated the principle in 2 Timothy 2:2 (TNIV): "The things you have heard me say in the presence of many witnesses entrust to reliable people who will also be qualified to teach others."

Who are some believers you know who would be receptive to a deeper relationship as well as encouragement and partnership in the area of evangelism?

## Inspire It

In his book *The Diffusion of Innovations*, Dr. Everett Rogers explains that innovative leaders are willing to travel outside of their normal circle to get new ideas and fresh inspiration.[10] Doing so expands their world, stretches their thinking, and lifts their vision, giving them a new perspective on their own situation.

Where could you go and where might you send other leaders and key influencers in your church to become inspired toward greater evangelistic vision and action? It might be by visiting an effective outreach-oriented church on the other side of town, or a high-powered evangelistic conference on the other side of the country (such as the annual National Outreach Convention sponsored by Outreach, Inc.[11]). As many leaders will testify, myself included, the dividends for making moderate investments in travel and training can be huge. Evangelistic fervor can be instilled in hearts and minds in rapid and powerful ways, sometimes impacting folks in several days in ways that might have taken months or years by just staying at home.

And if you're a leader or church member whose pastor could use a shot of evangelistic inspiration, sometimes a small investment in a conference registration, hotel, or transportation, along with a nudge of encouragement, can go a long way toward facilitating an experience that can reignite a heart for lost people.

Also, many church leadership teams have been inspired by reading this book, *Becoming a Contagious Church*, and discussing and debating its ideas each week, chapter by chapter.

## Personalize It

Most people are not moved by statistics or strategic initiatives alone; they need to see this issue on a more personal level — including how it might affect the people they care about most. For example, the new evangelism emphasis starts to seem really important when they think about their son, daughter, or grandchild who has lost all interest in the church and in spiritual matters. Or perhaps they are concerned about a parent, friend, coworker, or neighbor. When a loved one's life and eternity are at stake, levels of personal interest and motivation climb sharply.

Here is part of a letter from a woman who initially didn't want her church to change. Notice what moved her to express openness to fresh approaches:

> I would like to add my vote for having a regular contemporary worship service in our church. My husband and I have four kids who would greatly benefit from this type of service. Three of them will not attend a traditional service but have said they would attend a service that had "cool music." I have also talked with other people and invited them to church, but they think the traditional service is "too stiff and boring." I believe that if we are going to reach out to all of our community and the lost, we *have* to offer something more appealing to them, yet with the true gospel message. Please help this type of service happen at our church.

Helping church members see the benefits of new outreach approaches for their own loved ones is one of the best ways to begin to nurture and grow their hearts for evangelism more generally, as well.

## Fund It

A major step toward growing our hearts for people is opening our wallets for evangelism. Jesus said in Matthew 6:20–21: "Store up for yourselves treasures in heaven, where moth and rust do not destroy, and where thieves do not break in and steal. *For where your treasure is, there your heart will be also*" (emphasis added). Jesus is saying that as we invest more in this area, our hearts for people will grow accordingly.

And most churches certainly need to increase their level of investment in evangelism! George Barna reported in his book *Evangelism That Works* that "the average annual budget allocated by the typical church for all of its local evangelistic endeavors amounts to only about 2 percent of the gross annual revenues received by the church."[12] If we are going to become a contagious church, we need to invest well beyond that paltry level. Although it can be expensive, the money spent is truly an investment in the souls of men, women, and children, and it will lead to the future health and vitality of the church.

Where can you find enough money? First, *make the needs known, and expand this part of your regular budget.* If there is no section of the budget for evangelism or local missions, add one. Second, *ask key donors in your church to help you reach more lost people.* Wise kingdom investors are usually more than willing to give to evangelism, because they know it will bring lasting returns to people's eternities and to the church.

As they give—and as your church raises this as a priority in the budget—hearts for lost people will grow as well.

## Schedule It

Another investment that helps us deepen this value is actually committing our time to evangelism. This is true individually and churchwide. One of the best ways to ensure this happens is by scheduling dates on the church calendar, as well as reserving the rooms needed, so that outreach-oriented prayer times, training seminars, strategy sessions, team meetings, and outreach services and events can happen. It might also mean going on multiple-day trips to observe effective churches and ministries or to attend vision-lifting conferences and workshops.

Be warned about two things. First, conflict will occur when outreach needs compete with established programs designed to nurture believers. The catch–22 is that you need these training and outreach events, in part, to help build believers' hearts for evangelism. But what if there isn't enough heart there yet to make room for the events? My advice, distilled from some insightful teaching by Gene Appel, is to stretch them in the right direction, but don't push too far too fast. As people see the fruits of these efforts and feel the exhilaration of watching God work in the lives of their friends, their support will grow and they'll be ready to move further next time.[13]

A second warning: In scheduling outreach training and events, don't wait until you feel completely prepared. It will never happen! Motivational speaker and author Les Brown says that the key to growing and making changes is to "make your move before you are ready." It's like the challenge, "Leap and the net will appear!" I suppose this advice could be abused, but my experience tells me that when it comes to evangelism, it's usually right. God shows up, help comes through, details fall together, and people are impacted by the gospel—while commitment to evangelism deepens, in you and in the church!

## Measure It

We need to measure our evangelistic effectiveness so we'll know where we're making progress and where we need to put more effort. As the saying goes, "If you can't measure it, you can't manage it." Some opportunities for measuring include counting commitments to Christ, baptisms of new believers, attendance at outreach events, people in seeker small groups, people in training courses, and members involved with your evangelism team. You may want to track some or all of these factors.

As you're instilling values in the people around you, beware of the wrong benchmarks. The ultimate question is not whether your church is larger than it used to be or whether it's the biggest in town. When attendees at Willow Creek say to its leaders, "We already have thousands of people attending—isn't that enough?" their standard response is, "No, not as long as there are still nonbelievers within our reach!"

We have to aim high—Jesus says to go into *all* the world. We need to track progress so we know when to reexamine strategy or increase efforts, as well as when to celebrate success.

### Reinforce and Celebrate It

One of the most important but neglected ways to fight evangelistic entropy is to reinforce the good things that are happening by affirming the people who are in the middle of the action. We need to make heroes out of ordinary Christians who have had a contagious influence.

George Barna notes with surprise in *Evangelism That Works* that even among the most outreach-oriented churches there is a tendency to "recognize the evangelized but essentially ignore the evangelizers."[14] Obviously we need to be careful how we give recognition. We don't want to start giving out merit badges to those who have led the most people to Christ. But it's amazing how far acknowledgment and a word of thanks from a leader will go. This can be communicated through a note, a phone call, or perhaps a mention at an appropriate moment during a ministry gathering or worship service.

Some churches have begun to encourage friends and family to accompany new believers during baptism. Often this results in the person who was the primary influence standing in front of the church with the one being baptized — often while a testimony is given telling how God worked through him or her. This gives honor to the evangelizer while reinforcing evangelistic values in all who watch.

Those doing evangelism often feel like they're out there all alone, cut off from the centralized activity and fellowship of the church. It's vital that we affirm them and, in front of the entire congregation, underscore the importance of what they're doing.

And nothing fires up a Christian or a church more than seeing the tangible results of their evangelistic efforts in the form of new believers! So tell the stories, profile the testimonies, celebrate the changed lives, and expand on what God is doing in your midst.

## RESULTS OF INSTILLING EVANGELISTIC VALUES

When we "declare war" and apply these approaches to lift up evangelistic values in the church, three things tend to happen.

### 1. Most People Embrace the Values

Renewing your commitment to evangelism will deepen the value in the majority of the people in your church. When you and other leaders insist on emphasizing a biblical value like evangelism, and when listeners are committed to the life-changing truth of the Bible and are led by the

Holy Spirit, they generally respond over time with great enthusiasm. Gradually the evangelistic temperature rises in each person and in the church as a whole.

## 2. A Few People Resist the Values

Invariably, when you declare the mission, draw a line in the sand, and make some changes needed to reach more people, a few members will refuse to accept it. Some of them just need a bit more time. Change is hard for most people, but for some it is downright painful. We must be patient and empathetic, and realize that at times good people will say negative, reactionary things out of a fear of the unknown. Later some of them will be won back over, and they'll wish they hadn't reacted the way they did. A few of them may even become your strongest advocates and partners, and they'll thank you for standing firm on what the Bible says about the church and its evangelistic purpose.

But not all of them! For a variety of reasons, some people will be unable to go along with you and the other leaders in your efforts to reach people. They may like the broad concept, but not the methodology or the particular ministry style. In the long run, these people may be happier if they find another church that better fits them.

And some people won't even like the broad concept! I hate to say it as much as I hate to see it, but there are some people who profess to be Christians yet don't care one whit about people outside of God's family. They are typically self-centered and think the church revolves around them and exists solely to meet their needs. They probably wouldn't actually say it, but their attitude projects the message that they want what they want, and everyone else can go to hell — *literally.* These people need to be confronted for their sinful attitudes and called to repentance (Galatians 6:1). Hopefully they will turn around and begin to embrace God's heart of love for lost people. If this happens, everybody wins. But if they refuse, you must hold firmly to God's guidance and the priorities of his Word for your church.

Be advised, though, that if these people leave, they'll likely do so with a very different perception of reality than you and the other leaders in your church have. Some will be very vocal about what they may describe as you or your pastor's overbearing leadership, your unbiblical ideas, your compromise with the culture, or — fill in the blank. Some of what they say will probably shock you.

Listen to their complaints graciously, but avoid giving an immediate response. Search your heart to see if there's any grain of truth in what they're saying, and, if so, address it humbly. Then do your best to gently but firmly confront any errors or misrepresentations in what they are saying—and after that you must move on. Be patient, but don't get sidetracked. You have to keep your focus on the ministry God has given you.

## 3. New People Will Be Attracted Who Carry the Values

On the brighter side, an exciting phenomenon occurs when you lift up a vision and commitment to evangelism: New people who already *have* evangelistic hearts will be attracted to your church! Contagious Christians are looking for a church that is serious about reaching lost people, and when they find one, they are excited to join and then do their part to advance the cause.

A number of years ago, right after I'd first started working at Willow Creek, I heard a rumor that Marie Little had been visiting our services. Marie is the widow of Paul Little, the leader who wrote such books as *Know What You Believe* and *Know Why You Believe*, as well as the wonderful classic on personal evangelism, *How to Give Away Your Faith*.

The rumor turned out to be true, and I soon met with and became friends with Marie. She later told me that when she first started coming to our church, friends from her previous church were surprised that she would pick what seemed like such a youthful and raucous place. I'll never forget what she told me she said to them: "All I know is that people are getting *saved* over at Willow Creek—*and I've got to be where the action is!*" For nearly two decades, Marie Little has been one of the church's key volunteers and one of the brightest examples of church members who love lost people, as she has helped lead numerous people to Christ and discipled even more.

The point is not that we should try to recruit people from other churches—we didn't recruit Marie. What I'm saying is this: When a church turns up the heat on evangelism and says with its words and its actions, "We want to burn brightly with evangelistic intensity," it won't be able to keep evangelistically impassioned Christians from joining its ranks. They'll simply insist on "being where the action is!"

*Why can't that be your church?*

It can if you'll first live evangelistic values yourself, and then with God's help do all you can to instill those values in others around you.

You need to do this not only until there are a few more warm hearts for nonbelievers, but until there is a strong and growing evangelistic culture in your church. You'll know you have developed that kind of environment when caring for non-Christians becomes the norm, when increasing numbers of people are coming to faith, and when the mind-set of both leaders and members is to do whatever it takes to reach more and more people for Christ.

## STAGE 2: KEY IDEA

*The next step toward becoming a contagious church is instilling evangelistic values in others.*

> Hold to the standard of sound teaching that you have heard from me, in the faith and love that are in Christ Jesus.... And what you have heard from me through many witnesses entrust to faithful people who will be able to teach others as well. (2 Timothy 1:13; 2:2 NRSV)

# TO CONSIDER AND DISCUSS

1. What are some signs that a church has "declared war" when it comes to reaching people for Christ?

2. What will a church look like if its leaders fail to do what it takes to lift and uphold this vital value of evangelism?

3. How can you get help spreading evangelistic values in your church?

4. How can you invest more time and energy in praying for nonbelievers and encourage others to do the same?

5. When you consider your church's calendar and budgets, how do you think it is doing in terms of prioritizing evangelism?

6. What one or two scheduling or budgeting changes would you suggest to help your church raise its evangelistic effectiveness?

7. What do you know about, or what could you do to learn about, the evangelistic hopes of the men and women who originally planted your church? How could you communicate their desires to encourage the church today in this area?

8. Where are pockets of strength or signs of evangelistic impact within your church that should be identified and celebrated?

# CHAPTER FOUR

# STAGE 3: EMPOWER AN EVANGELISM LEADER

I WAS FEELING GOOD. I had just poured out my heart for a day and a half to a gathering of attentive senior pastors at an East Coast conference. They seemed to have real hearts for non-Christians and appeared to connect well with the principles I shared. I had encouraged them to do what it takes to keep their passion levels high for evangelism, and I had talked about the importance of instilling this value in the people around them—especially their fellow leaders. I'd also presented practical ideas for training their members to share their faith and for doing innovative outreach ministries and events.

If you're a speaker, you know that some days you're on, and some days you're not. Well I've gotta admit it: this felt like an *on* day! When the sessions were over, I got plenty of encouragement and positive feedback, and I felt confident the conference would rejuvenate evangelism in many of their churches.

What happened next burst my bubble.

## A RUDE AWAKENING

The pastor who had arranged for me to speak and hosted me at the conference mentioned that he'd have to drop me off at the airport a few minutes early. He said he needed to do a hospital visit before going back to his office for final preparations on the sermon for the next morning.

"A hospital visit?" I asked. "Is somebody in your church sick?"

He smiled. "Someone in our church is *always* sick," he said. "We have an aging congregation, so I'm constantly making trips to the hospital."

"And," I said, hoping for a more encouraging answer, "how many other people are on the ministry team that visits people in the hospital?"

"Just me," he said. "I've tried to involve other people, but our members really want—and expect—an appearance from the pastor. So I'm doing visitations almost daily. On top of that, there are all the funerals I have to do—about thirty last year alone!"

"Thirty funerals—all by yourself?" I asked with amazement, starting to feel a bit uneasy. "So you must not do all of the teaching on Sunday mornings, right? Do you have a team of teachers who preach on a rotating basis?"

He looked surprised. "I'm the *pastor*," he said patiently. "I do all of the preaching, not just every Sunday morning but also every Sunday night and every Wednesday night. I'm up front teaching three times a week."

"My goodness!" I exclaimed. "How in the world do you keep up with preparing and delivering three messages a week, a funeral every other week, and a hospital visitation almost every day?" Then I just couldn't stop myself from asking another question: "You don't do the weddings too, do you?"

At this point he gave me a look that said, *You just don't seem to get it, son!*

"Yes, I do the weddings, as well as the premarital counseling—not to mention marriage counseling later if there are problems," he said. "And to tell you the truth, it's really tough keeping up with my ministry and trying to be a good husband and father in my own family too."

"I'm seeing that," I said, my mind reeling. *And*, I thought to myself, *there's not a chance in the world that he—or any of the other pastors in similar situations—will be able to find the time or energy to employ the ideas I taught at the conference the last couple of days. They left with great intentions, but they simply can't do it all.*

## LESSONS LEARNED

That day marked me. It left me with three distinct impressions. The first was a deepened respect for the many faithful pastors who deserve honor for the incredible efforts they put into their ministries day after day, week after week, year after year. The next time we're ready to criticize something the pastor did or did not do, we need to slow down and extend some grace. We need to honor those who so steadfastly serve us. As Paul says in 1 Timothy 5:17, "The elders who direct the affairs of the church well are worthy of double honor, especially those whose work is preaching and teaching."

My second impression, however, was that the church as a whole needs to get back to a more biblically defined way of doing ministry. We claim to believe in "the priesthood of all believers." Many churches even put it in print with statements like, "We have one pastor but many ministers," implying that every member is actually serving in a ministry position.

This *sounds* good, but look around. Is it true? Often the reality is that there is one person who is both pastor and minister, and then there are many helpers. These helpers are assigned to limited and often menial roles, while the pastor is nearly dying trying to keep up with all of the real ministry functions. This approach will nearly (and in some cases, *actually*) kill the pastor, and it will limit the quality and quantity of the ministry happening in and around the church. It will also squelch the spiritual passion and potential of the members who are being limited in the use of their spiritual gifts and the scope of their ministry impact. Romans 12:3–6 says:

> For by the grace given me I say to every one of you: Do not think of yourself more highly than you ought, but rather think of yourself with sober judgment, in accordance with the measure of faith God has given you. Just as each of us has one body with many members, and these members do not all have the same function, so in Christ we who are many form one body, and each member belongs to all the others. We have different gifts, according to the grace given us.

It's time to start letting all the members express themselves and their gifts in meaningful ways. But, as you know, change is not easy. It requires the teaching—and gradual acceptance—of a whole new set of expectations. For example, people need to understand that when they're in the hospital, they will be visited by those in their closest circle of fellowship, and then, additionally, by a volunteer member from the church's pastoral care team. This person should have the gifts, passion, training, time, and energy to make the visit. Possessing these qualities, combined with sheer availability, means he or she can generally minister much more effectively than the pastor could have.

Who wins in this equation? *Everybody!*

The hurting people win because they are ministered to by people who can focus on serving them. The ministering people win because they experience the joy, fulfillment, and affirmation that come with serving according to their gifts. The pastor wins because he can concentrate on his primary roles. And, consequently, the whole church wins because all members can now be better led and taught.

Remember how the early church followed this pattern in Acts 6:2–5?

> The Twelve gathered all the disciples together and said, "It would not be right for us to neglect the ministry of the word of God in order to wait on tables. Brothers, choose seven men from among you who are known to be full of the Spirit and wisdom. We will turn this responsibility over to them and will give our attention to prayer and the ministry of the word." This proposal pleased the whole group.

And what were the results of this decision? This is what Acts 6:7 says:

> The word of God spread. The number of disciples in Jerusalem increased rapidly, and a large number of priests became obedient to the faith.

In short, this biblical approach to dividing the labor frees leaders and pastors—like the one sitting across from me that day—to better live out evangelistic values and then instill them in the people in their church.

I realize I've opened a huge subject here, but it's a vitally important one if we're to become contagious—or, for that matter, healthy—churches. For further reading, I recommend *What You Do Best in the Body of Christ* by Bruce Bugbee[1] and *The New Reformation: Returning the Ministry to the People of God* by Greg Ogden.[2] More than that, I urge you to use a program such as the updated *Network* training curriculum, developed by Bruce Bugbee and Don Cousins.[3] It is a six-hour course that will, if taught repeatedly over time, help all your members discover their God-given spiritual gifts, ministry passion, and personal ministry styles so that they can be placed in appropriate ministry positions.

This leads to the third thing that struck me that day: Most of the big ideas about making a church evangelistically effective are never going to materialize if we are relying on senior pastors to do all of the work. Instead, *we need to select and empower a leader who will partner with the pastor in championing the evangelism cause* and then lead the way in implementing a strategic outreach plan.

## THE MISSING PERSON

In keeping with our "declare war" motif, let's look at what Robert McNamara, the United States secretary of defense (who served in the administrations of presidents Kennedy and Johnson), said in his book, *In Retrospect*, about a leadership mistake made by the U.S. government during the Vietnam War.

> No senior person in Washington dealt *solely* with Vietnam.... We should have established a full-time team at the highest level— what Churchill called a War Cabinet—focused on Vietnam and nothing else.... It should have met weekly with the president at prescribed times for long, uninterrupted discussions.... The meetings should have been characterized by the openness and candor of the Executive Committee deliberations during the Cuban Missile Crisis—which contributed to the avoidance of a catastrophe.[4]

Did you catch that? No single individual was in charge of figuring out what the United States should do during the Vietnam conflict. What a shocking revelation!

Bill Hybels applied this illustration at a Leadership Summit:

> Some of us do the same thing. We say we need a thrust in the area of evangelism. So we talk about it, we identify it, but we never assign it to a person. We never say, "Look—we're going to ask you to put this as the front-burner item on your job description. We need you to lead us up that hill. Here's the path; here are some mile markers; we're going to meet back regularly to see that you're making progress." Friends, if you don't do that, you're going to be in trouble. You won't make the progress you want to make.
>
> If pastors are going to juggle multiple challenges, the challenges must be identified and prioritized. Then someone has to carry the ball. Someone has to be thinking full-time, either on a lay-level or a paid-staff basis, about just that one challenge. This person needs to be pulling in teams around himself or herself in order to make progress.

We also have to manage the progress of these people. We have to evaluate the rate, the process, the strategies, and the achievements of these thrusts that we're trying to make. Are things moving quickly enough? Are they moving too slowly? Are the problems being solved appropriately? Do we need more resources or more expertise? It has to be managed to the point of effectiveness.

Using a different metaphor, my friend Karl Singer, a leader in the financial services industry for many years, said it to me like this: "Any business that wants to succeed over the long haul must do two things really well: First, give great service to its present customers; and second, constantly acquire new customers." Then, with characteristic frankness, Karl looked me in the eye and asked, "So why is it that most churches—churches that *say* they want to prevail for generations to come—don't have *anyone* in charge of acquiring new business? If they're serious about surviving in the future, they're going to have to find and equip the missing person whose job it will be to reach people outside the church."

## STRATEGIC MINISTRY REQUIRES STRATEGIC LEADERSHIP

Can you imagine a church without a head of children's ministry? *Somebody* has to be responsible for the care and teaching of the children. What about students? It is almost inconceivable that a church would try to function without a youth minister. And adult education? If church leaders take seriously Jesus' mandate to teach people to obey everything he has commanded us (see Matthew 28:20), they must put someone in charge of adult education. Just go down the list: music directors, worship leaders, choir directors, Sunday school superintendents, camp directors. Whenever a ministry is deemed important, somebody is put in charge of it. That person may be a paid staff member or a committed volunteer, but if the ministry really matters, you'll be able to find a name on it!

Yet in most churches you'll find no name when it comes to evangelism. Or there may be several names but no one really responsible. Or there may be one name, but outreach is just one of six or eight "priorities" on that person's job description—and it generally falls to the bottom of the list. Or the senior pastor may claim to be in charge of evangelism. As I've shown earlier, the pastor must be involved, especially at the broader leadership and vision level (especially in Stages 1 and 2), but the pastor will never find the time to start and manage everything needed to make a church truly contagious.

That's why Stage 3 of our 6-Stage Process says we must "EMPOWER an Evangelism Leader." We need to find someone who has the right mix of gifts, experience, and abilities. He or she must be given the freedom to focus. Call the role Director of Evangelism, Pastor of Evangelism, Associate Pastor of Outreach, or whatever creative title you come up with, but I'm convinced that every church ought to appoint and empower someone to fill this vital role, and I believe that Ephesians 4:11 – 12 supports this when it says: "It was he who gave some ... to be evangelists ... to prepare God's people for works of service, so that the body of Christ may be built up."

When possible, the evangelism leader should be a paid staff member so that he or she can spend sufficient time each day furthering the cause. If the church cannot afford to pay this person (as will often be the case, at least initially), then find the best volunteer leader you possibly can. Challenge that person to give the position everything they've got. As seekers are reached and the support base of the church grows, the position might naturally expand into a staff role.

You might be thinking, *This must be a "big church" concept; at our level, we could never think of having someone focus just on evangelism.*

Well, big churches do need an evangelistic point person, but so do smaller churches—perhaps even more so. Often in smaller churches much of the work is done by one person, the pastor, and there is very little division of labor. Intentional evangelism, therefore, with all of its challenges and demands, typically gets relegated to a later time. "We're already overwhelmed just keeping up with meeting the needs of our small congregation," the logic goes. "I can't imagine how hard it would be if we started getting a bunch of new people to join us!"

This situation never improves much on its own. Five or ten years later, the pastor is *still* trying to keep up with meeting the needs of the members—and the church has become deeply entrenched in its inward focus. The key is to start implementing division of labor now—regardless of your church's size—and to view newcomers not so much as people the church will need to serve but more as potential members who will soon serve and support the church. This mind-set, combined with taking the vital step of empowering the right person to take the evangelistic lead, can begin to revolutionize your church and its potential for future growth and impact.

## THE MISSING PERSON PROFILE

Identifying the right leader may not be easy. What does he or she look like? Although it's hard to paint a comprehensive picture, let me list some important attributes under the broad headings of *character*, *competency*, and *chemistry*. You won't find all of these to the same degree in any one person, but I'd proceed with great caution if any are weak or missing.

### Character

- Unquestioned integrity and reputation
- Authentic walk with Christ
- Heart for lost people
- Passion for the truth of Scripture
- Courageous and persevering

### Competency

- Proven leadership skills; strategist, organizer, and communicator
- Projects a vision for limitless kingdom growth
- Track record of impacting seekers for Christ
- Strong desire to equip others for evangelistic impact
- Able to define and defend Christian doctrine

### Chemistry

- Strong affinity with the senior pastor
- Relates well to a broad range of personalities
- Works with and can accomplish goals through teams
- Open to the ideas and evangelistic styles of others
- Has an enthusiastic vision-lifting influence with the church

## FINDING THE MISSING PERSON

Where do we find this missing person?

Apply the first two stages in our 6-Stage Process: (1) LIVE evangelism values, and (2) INSTILL those values in others. Keep holding the banner high, and make it clear that *this is a church that will be known for its evangelistic passion.* Often the right leader will surface or just show up. But if not, you'll have to look for one. Start within your own congregation, but don't assume that the person in your church who is "known for doing evangelism" is the right person. You need a leader and a people-person who relates well to a broad range of personality types. Sometimes strong evangelists are admired for their zeal—but avoided for their approach! They might be regarded as a bit fanatical. When they talk about evangelism, others discount what they say because, after all, "That's just 'Fired-Up-Charlie,' and he is *always* talking about that stuff."

Another danger is that a current leader may be locked into one particular approach to evangelism and tend to project it onto everybody in the church. This will attract a few people who happen to fit that approach, but it will repel everyone else. A vital part of enrolling *all* the believers in the church is a strong belief that there are *many* valid ways to do evangelism (we'll discuss this further in the next chapter). This principle must be taught wholeheartedly and then applied consistently throughout the evangelism ministries and events.

For example, someone who presently leads a visitation team may or may not be able to make the leap to embrace and espouse a variety of other legitimate options. If he or she can, this person may be the right evangelism leader for your church. If not, this person may still be a key player leading a certain niche of evangelism under the direction of the new leader.

Don't assume that the leader must be a flamboyant extrovert who is always the life of the party, or of a particular age, or look like an evangelist (whatever that means!). Beware, too, of assuming the leader has to be someone with a formal degree in biblical studies or evangelism. That can be a definite asset, but it doesn't have to be a prerequisite. And in some cases it can bring with it the limiting viewpoint of "the way things should be done according to such and such a book or Professor So-and-So." Sometimes the most creative and effective leaders are those who take up the challenge but who "really don't have the background for it." This may be just the person to put into active duty, and then give him or her additional training—formal or informal—along the way.

Carrying this thought a bit further, avoid thinking that this leader has to be someone with many years of experience in evangelism—which will severely limit your slate of candidates and diminish the value of on-the-job training. One of the most effective people I know in local church evangelism was recruited straight out of the marketplace by the same church God had used to reach him just a few years earlier. Look for sharp leaders throughout your ministries who have a concern for lost people and an affinity with people on both sides of the spiritual fence. Set a higher goal for character than for breadth of evangelistic experience. It's always easier to develop skills than it is to build character.

If necessary, look outside your church for an evangelism leader. A local or denominational Bible college or seminary can be a good resource, as long as the selection is based on the criteria we've been discussing. Sometimes by networking with other church leaders you'll find that they have someone in their ranks who fits the description but who, for any number of reasons, they have been unable to fully utilize. For the sake of kingdom gain, ask them if they will "trade" that leader with the awareness that their church gets to have the first-round draft choice the next time around!

You might even come into contact with someone who has become frustrated trying to create evangelistic action in another church but has found it unmovable. You'll probably discover that both the person and that church's leaders are frustrated about it. Perhaps everyone would win if this evangelistic pioneer had an opportunity to put his or her energy into a different church that really wants to try some new things to reach people—yours!

A couple of final thoughts about finding the right leader to head up the evangelism thrust in your church: First, *pray specifically and consistently.* The former associate pastor of Willow Creek, Don Cousins, used to remind me that Jesus went into the desert to fast and pray before selecting his disciples (Matthew 4). We should follow Jesus' example, because this is a critically important decision. Seek God's guidance and protection as you select a leader. Second, *set your sights high.* People may come across your path about whom you'll think, *if only ...,* but you'll be tempted to skip pursuing them because you don't think they would be interested. Listen: don't say *no* for them before they have a chance to say *yes!* Let them catch a glimpse of the vision for and importance of the role you have in mind. Then they can prayerfully decide if they're interested in signing up for the most exciting adventure of their life!

I've seen highly successful people in the marketplace begin to see how God can use them and, in the words of the Steven Curtis Chapman song, they "abandon it all for the sake of the call." I know one businessman who left his role as a corporate executive, accepted a 90 percent pay cut, and got involved in full-time ministry. Not only that—he now gives more money to the ministry than he actually makes working there! (But don't ask me for his name and number—I won't give it to you!)

Don't limit God. And don't shrink back from challenging the person you think is right for this role. He or she is going to be in charge of "new business," which represents the future of the church and the eternal destiny of everyone who will be reached. What could possibly be more important than this?

## THE EVANGELISM LEADER'S JOB DESCRIPTION

The evangelism leader's role is to champion the 6-Stage Process, especially Stages 4 through 6, which we'll discuss in the following chapters. In the case of the first three stages, his or her efforts should supplement those of the pastor and other leaders and influencers who have already grasped the vision for becoming a contagious church. Here's a quick look at how this should work, along with a short preview of the final three stages:

### The Evangelism Leader's Supplementary Role

#### Stage 1: LIVE an Evangelistic Life

In addition to the pastor and other key staff and volunteers, people will naturally look to the evangelism leader to be an example of someone who cares deeply about lost people and takes practical steps to reach them. This should provide extra motivation for the person in this role. Every time the leader takes a risk in a relationship or conversation with a non-Christian, he or she has the opportunity to impact that person's eternity—as well as to encourage and influence the Christians who are watching.

Like the rest of us, this person needs to have some space for inevitable evangelistic ups and downs. As long as the overall desire and effort to reach others is strong, the people in the congregation can learn from and be motivated by this leader's example—which includes the ongoing personal fight against evangelistic entropy and the battle to overcome discouragement when outreach efforts don't go as planned.

#### Stage 2: INSTILL Evangelistic Values in the People around You

The evangelism leader should take a strong partnering role with the senior pastor in raising evangelism values in the church. They can declare war together! A natural synergy will form as they inspire, encourage, and hold one another accountable, and pray for each other.

Ecclesiastes 4:9 – 10 really applies here when it says:

> Two are better than one, because they have a good return for their
> work:
> If one falls down, his friend can help him up.
> But pity the man who falls and has no one to help him up!

### Stage 3: EMPOWER *Additional* Evangelism Leaders

Part of the evangelism leader's job is to find and equip other leaders
who can come alongside and help carry out the evangelism plan. Most
of these people should remain in the various ministries throughout the
church, but ally with the main evangelism leader to help lift outreach
values and activity within the various ministries.

That's why the evangelism leader must be a high-level leader of leaders. The job is too big to handle alone. This is a real war, and wars require
leadership, teamwork, creativity, planning, and courage. In the power
of the Holy Spirit, we need to mount a massive counterattack to weaken
the enemy, take back lost ground, and reclaim the captives—the church
*must* prevail!

While the evangelism leader should come alongside the pastor and
the other leaders on the first three stages, the last three are the *primary*
responsibilities of that leader.

## The Evangelism Leader's Primary Role

How are we going to make this evangelistic strategy work throughout the
church? By continuing our 6-Stage Process. Stages 4 through 6 make up
the primary day-to-day activities—a three-part job description—of the
evangelism leader. Here's a very brief overview of those three stages; we'll
go into greater depth on each one in the next three chapters.

### Stage 4: TRAIN the Church in Evangelism Skills—The 100 Percent

People don't develop skills just by hearing an inspiring talk or by watching
other people model those skills. They learn by practicing the skills themselves. One of the first and most important jobs of the evangelism leader
is to implement training (whether in seminars, classes and small groups,
churchwide campaigns, or all of the above) that can help every believer in
the church develop the skills and confidence to communicate their faith
to others. This is an ongoing job, because new people keep needing to be

trained, and those who have been trained need to come back for refreshers. We'll look at the training challenge in detail in chapter five.

### Stage 5: MOBILIZE the Church's Evangelism Specialists — The 10 Percent

One of the advantages of offering ongoing training is that it gives the evangelism leader and his or her team endless opportunities to identify and recruit those with gifts or passion in this area — people whose roles are vital in order to succeed. These are the folks to invite to occasional rallies designed to charge up their evangelistic batteries and alert them to upcoming outreach opportunities and training events. When the leader gets this group of enthusiasts together, momentum really starts building and things start getting fun! In chapter six we'll look at how to build and lead a diverse evangelism team.

### Stage 6: UNLEASH an Array of Outreach Ministries and Events

Once the evangelism leader has rallied a cross-departmental evangelism team, he or she now has the needed human resources from which to launch a wide range of outreach ministries and events. These are the people who will help the leader dream and determine what else should be done to try to reach lost people — and then make it happen. Remember, they "want to be where the action is!"

When, with God's help, you've laid the groundwork with Stages 1 through 5, and have begun to unleash Stage 6, *watch out!* The sky is the limit concerning what can happen in terms of evangelistic impact. We'll explore Stage 6 and look at some examples of what churches are doing in chapter seven.

## MAKING THE EVANGELISM LEADER POSITION WORK

I think it would be impossible to overstate the importance and potential of what we've talked about in this chapter. Since these ideas were originally published in an earlier version of this book and I started speaking on them at leadership conferences and seminars around the world, I've gotten more feedback from leaders about this concept of empowering an evangelism leader as "a partner to the pastor" than any other in the book. "It's been revolutionary," they'll tell me, "once we got the right person in the evangelism leadership role and got behind it ... it energized everything else we were trying to do evangelistically."

I sincerely hope you and the leaders at your church will prayerfully select and empower the right person, and begin seeing such dramatic results in your own setting. Regardless of your church's size, style, or setting, I'm convinced this will make a major difference.

Here are a few final thoughts on making this stage really succeed:

## EVANGELISM REQUIRES RESOURCES

As I hinted earlier, becoming a contagious church has costs associated with it. Even if your evangelism leader is a volunteer, you still need to provide some training, perhaps in the form of courses taken locally or by correspondence. You'll want to send this leader to occasional evangelism and leadership conferences to expand his or her vision, and to workshops to deepen skills and multiply contacts with like-minded contagious leaders. You'll also want this person to have access to good outreach-oriented books and recordings. And he or she will need a budget for phone calls, office expenses, and meetings and meals with other leaders, team members, and spiritual seekers.

Then when this leader starts training the church and building the churchwide evangelism team, you'll incur more expenses. Some of those can be recouped by charging participants nominal fees for meals and materials. But if you try to run your training and various outreach events on a strict break-even basis, you're going to restrict creativity and opportunities.

But going back to Karl Singer's illustration, why wouldn't we be willing to invest in the part of our organization that is in charge of "new business"? If you have to skimp somewhere, Singer would tell you, skimp somewhere else but not in the area that can breathe new life into every segment of the organization—not to mention bringing new life to the people you'll reach!

You may be wondering how much the evangelism budget will need to be expanded. Looking at the studies, the difference may be substantial (though not necessarily all at once). As we saw earlier, George Barna found that the average church spends less than 2 percent of total revenues on local evangelism. No wonder the war effort isn't going very well! But in comparison, Barna indicates that "among the *leading* evangelistic churches, we found that it was more common to spend 10 percent to 20 percent of the annual budget for that purpose.... In general, the churches that are most serious about evangelism seem to put their money where their mission is."[5]

Barna cautions, however, against the mentality that money alone produces results. He also asserts, "For a ministry that has creative thinkers, passionate evangelists, strong leaders, and wise strategists, providing a significant budget for evangelism can multiply the other gifts and abilities residing within the church many times over."[6]

Before leaving this topic, I want to address the issue of churches investing large amounts in foreign missions yet almost completely neglecting the lost people in their own community. Why is this often the case? Is it because it is easier to write a check than to get involved personally? Is it a spiritualized way of saying, "I'll let someone else do the work of evangelism for me"? Do we think that people on the other side of the ocean matter more to God than the people who live next door?

Please don't misunderstand me. I'm an enthusiastic and active supporter of foreign missions. I realize that evangelism is absolutely essential in other countries too. In many cases these ministries reach people who've never had the chance to hear the gospel. In addition, these people often live in incredibly needy areas where food, water, medicine, and shelter—as well as books, schools, teachers, and training—are sorely lacking. We who have been blessed with so much should give consistently and sacrificially to lighten these burdens and to reach people for Christ.

But we also have a responsibility to address the spiritual needs of those near us. In fact, some would say this is a biblical priority, based on Acts 1:8. Jesus said, "You will be my witnesses in Jerusalem, and in all Judea and Samaria, and to the ends of the earth." I don't want to argue that this command should be carried out in a sequential manner, with the mandate to thoroughly reach our "Jerusalem," or local area, before we move outward. But neither do I want to act like any part of it is optional! We have no business deciding to reach our Judea or Samaria *instead* of our Jerusalem. Yet this is often done, and our own children and grandchildren pay the price.

I heard about a large adult class in a vibrant evangelical church where the teacher became especially vulnerable one Sunday morning. With tears in his eyes he admitted that his own children had long since refused to attend their church because they couldn't relate to it. According to my friends who were there, many other class members came up to this man afterward and told him that the same was true of their own kids. Clearly, they wanted to change things and to figure out ways to invest in more relevant ministry and outreach. Yet their church's budget from the previous ministry year showed that they had spent less than 1 percent on local evangelism. Thankfully, this church's leadership has recognized the problem, and they are taking steps to turn things around and raise the priority of reaching their own community—while continuing to support overseas missions.

Consider whether in your church enough is being invested in ministries that can reach your own children as well as your friends and neighbors who don't know Christ. In a broad sense, the strong warning of 1 Timothy 5:8 applies here: "If anyone does not provide for his relatives, and especially for his immediate family, he has denied the faith and is worse than an unbeliever."

What can be done to increase funding for local evangelism? As with everything else related to evangelism, it starts with the heart. As we lift up this value and then put it into action along the lines of our discussion in this book, people will be moved to give the necessary finances. The goal is to increase the overall support and investment level for evangelism without harming other important causes. Also, you may have people in your congregation who, if you went to them personally and presented your plan, would joyfully write a check to help make it happen—especially when they consider the potential effects on their own loved ones!

You may also need to reallocate some of the funds that have been going elsewhere in the church. Lifting the value of evangelism will often raise it up higher on the priority scale than other ministry areas, and this should be reflected by levels of financial investment. But don't forget it's just that—an *investment* in lost people and in your church's future. As by God's grace it brings returns in the form of reenergized believers as well as freshly redeemed seekers, the base of investors will grow, and even more outreach will become possible.

## THE EVANGELISM LEADER MUST BE EMPOWERED

With the deep-seated resistance to evangelism we find so often, it is vital that the pastor and other senior leaders do all they can to *empower* the person who is leading the evangelism cause. This needs to be done initially, and then reinforced periodically, in vision talks that clarify the church's evangelistic mission—and that explain the strategic importance of the evangelism leader and his or her role in helping to fulfill that mission. It's critically important to actively include that leader up front in the service, letting him or her at least say a few words about the plans being developed.

The congregation needs to clearly see that the pastor and leaders are placing a mantle of leadership, trust, and authority on this person, enabling him or her to effectively guide and coach the church toward fulfilling its redemptive potential. George Barna writes, "One of the marks of effective leadership is the ability to identify qualified people, to prepare them for action and to release them to do what they do best with not just verbal blessings but with the mandate to do what is necessary to get the job done."[7]

Empowerment also comes through providing for regular interaction with the other leaders. This can be accomplished, in part, by adding this person to the leadership team and inviting him or her to the appropriate elder, deacon, or board meetings, depending on your church's structure. (Note: If red flags are going up in your mind right now, and you're realizing that the person you were considering doesn't have the clout or stature to run in those circles, then you need to reassess who should be filling this role in your church. You must find a leader who has, or who can quickly attain, that level of respect.)

This person must be given a measure of authority with other ministry leaders in the church, as evangelism cuts across all of the ministries. If your evangelism leader becomes just another leader in one of many departments in the church, then you've already positioned him or her to lose. Evangelism is the razor's edge of what your church claims to be all about; you must treat it that way!

Another key to empowerment is to free up this leader to focus on evangelism. Don't load up his or her job description with activities like weddings, funerals, unnecessary meetings and retreats, or too many teaching responsibilities. In particular, beware of making this leader the "Director of Evangelism *and Discipleship*." (If you think about it, that's pretty much everything the church does! Plus, discipleship usually requires shepherding gifts, which from my experience very few evangelism leaders tend to have.) Be aware that, as the old saying goes, "the squeaky wheel gets the grease" — and spiritual seekers out in your community almost never "squeak"! Who squeaks? It's usually needy believers who are constantly clamoring for more and more attention. When you add other roles to the evangelism leader's job description, these will inevitably compete with — and far too often overcome — the role of leading the church's evangelistic charge. Again, the word is *focus*.

## THE EVANGELISM LEADER MUST BE ACCOUNTABLE

In spite of these warnings and your efforts to keep the evangelism leader focusing in the right areas, he or she can easily get sidetracked — not necessarily doing bad things, but lower-priority things. Accountability needs to be built in to make sure this person is concentrating on the agreed-upon goals.

One of the easiest places for this leader to get off track is to begin responding personally to all of the cries for help in the evangelism arena. These can come from non-Christians or, more often, from church members who want personalized help in reaching their friends and family. Certainly some of these should be dealt with directly by the leader; he or she should never become isolated from that kind of direct ministry. But, on the whole, evangelism leaders should see themselves as facilitators whose main role is to equip and enroll others in the front lines of ministry action — others who they help develop to respond to the various outreach opportunities. It's interesting that the Bible passage I quoted earlier, Ephesians 4:11–12, indicates that the role of the person who fills what is often referred to as the "office of evangelist" is not supposed to do the evangelism *for* the church but, rather, "*to prepare God's people* for works of service, so that the body of Christ may be built up" (emphasis mine).

I've met evangelism leaders who buoyantly tell me how many people they've personally led to Christ in the past year. The number is always impressive. But my reaction is invariably mixed. On the one hand, I'm thankful that God is using them to reach so many. On the other, I wonder how much more fruitful their long-term effect might be if instead of handling all of these situations themselves, they were doing more of what that verse says: empowering other Christians and leading them into opportunities in which they could get a taste of the excitement of bringing someone to Christ.

Sharing the responsibility with others would ignite and embolden every one of these Christians and make them that much more able to be used in evangelism again and again. That's because when a believer leads another person to Christ, they instantly gain so much more confidence in the power of the gospel, the presence of the Holy Spirit, and the potential of their evangelistic efforts. Soon they lead another person to Christ. And then another. And another.

Here's a different way of looking at what I've learned:

## 1 x 100 is less than 100 x 1

What this means is that one person leading a hundred others to faith is not nearly as great as that same person helping one hundred others to each lead one other person to faith. Why? Because in the second scenario, you not only end up with a hundred new believers, you also have a hundred newly fired-up evangelists who now know the exhilaration and fulfillment of leading someone else to Christ! They've gotten past the awkward insecure stage, and they're gaining increased confidence and excitement about communicating their faith to others. They will, as a result, be much more likely to lead more and more people into God's family.

By acting primarily as a facilitator and coach, the evangelism leader is investing in the exponential effects of empowering ever-increasing numbers of Christians who will each reach others. In short, the church will be becoming contagious!

## THE EVANGELISM LEADER MUST BE ENCOURAGED

The evangelism leader is a servant who helps lead the church into battle. Frustration, discouragement, and times of weariness are all periodic by-products of this arena of ministry, especially since spiritual battles are continually being waged. Thus, this brother or sister in Christ needs prayer, love, support, understanding, encouragement, and appreciation—especially from other leaders in the church. Often just a little bit will go a long way.

A well-chosen evangelism leader will be able to steer your church into fruitful ministry at many different levels—attacking on many fronts and, over time, helping your church to win the war and spiritually impact more and more people. Every church—large, small, or even in the initial planting stage—needs to identify and empower this kind of leader. Then this person can begin to train and empower the rest of the members to reach their lost friends for Christ. We'll look at how this can happen in the next chapter.

## STAGE 3: KEY IDEA

*Empower a contagious leader who will be able to train, mobilize, and lead many others for evangelism.*

It was he who gave some ... to be evangelists ... to prepare God's people for works of service, so that the body of Christ may be built up. (Ephesians 4:11–12)

# TO CONSIDER AND DISCUSS

1. How would it help your church to have an evangelism leader to champion this cause in partnership with the senior pastor and other leaders?

2. How could your pastor and the evangelism leader best work in tandem with each other?

3. If you don't yet have somebody in this role, who are two or three people inside or outside your church that might make an effective evangelism leader? Begin praying for wisdom concerning who is the right person for this vital area.

4. Why is it essential for the evangelism leader to be freed up to focus on recruiting, training, and deploying more people in this ministry?

5. If your church already has an evangelism leader in place, what can you do to strengthen this person to make him or her even more effective?

# CHAPTER FIVE

# STAGE 4: TRAIN THE CHURCH IN EVANGELISM SKILLS—THE 100 PERCENT

WE'VE GOT A SERIOUS MATH *problem.*

Go into many churches and ask the pastor, "In your church, whose job is it to do evangelism?" You'll likely get a sincere reply along the lines of: "Oh, that's primarily the role of the people in the congregation. If you look at the biblical model, it shows that I'm the shepherd and they're the flock. But shepherds can't make sheep; the *sheep* have to make sheep! My job is to equip the flock and send them out to do the work of evangelism."

This might sound pretty good—until you discover how few people in most churches are being adequately equipped to communicate their faith to others. Of the churches that do train their people, most do so infrequently, teach just one approach, and have a relatively low number of members who actually participate. Is it any wonder the job isn't getting done?

What's worse, if you talk to most church members, they will often give you a very different answer to the question about whose job evangelism is. With great buoyancy they'll reply, "Oh, that's the *pastor's* job. The pastor is the one with the special training and skills and equipment and whatever else it takes. Why would I jeopardize someone's eternity when there's a paid professional around who is much more qualified to help them?"

I call this "evangelistic finger pointing": pastors pointing at their congregations, and their congregations pointing back at them. Sometimes this finger pointing becomes even more creative. Somebody will remember that, according to the experts, as many as 10 percent of Christians have the spiritual gift of evangelism. "Of course," they'll say, "*that's* whose job evangelism is—the people with the gift! God made it easy for them and hard for the rest of us. We'll just support their efforts!"

But the question is, *who* are they? *Where* are they? Imagine standing in front of your church this Sunday morning and saying, "We know that about one in ten of you have the spiritual gift of evangelism. We'd like to find out who you are. No big deal; we'll just jot down your names and get back to you later. Could those of you with the evangelism gift please stand?" What kind of a response do you think you'd get? Would anywhere near 10 percent of the congregation be standing? Maybe 5 percent? Perhaps only 2 percent—or even less?

Let's be honest. In most churches, the actual number of people who would stand and say, "Evangelism is my gift area," is extremely small. Of those few who would make that claim, many are undertrained and ill prepared. And let's be even more honest: Some of them are offbeat characters you would not want representing your church and upon whom you could never build an effective outreach effort!

See why I say we have a math problem? We have billions of people in the world who don't know Christ—and probably thousands near your church. And most of our congregations have, at best, a small handful of motivated and equipped believers—with or without the spiritual gift of evangelism—to do the actual reaching. It's no surprise that in so many quarters the church is losing ground or merely maintaining the status quo. And it's no wonder Jesus so earnestly challenged his followers, "The harvest is plentiful, but the workers are few. Ask the Lord of the harvest, therefore, to send out workers into his harvest field" (Luke 10:2).

## THE MATH PROBLEM HITS HOME

This situation is, for me, more than mere theory. At one time I was a casualty of this math problem. In fact, I reached the point of actually writing off personal evangelism and deciding it wasn't for me at all!

Why? It was the fallout of a summer of evangelism overseas. I had been on a team with a wonderful church that was trying to share Christ with people in its neighborhoods. The problem was that they were using approaches that didn't fit my personality. I remember asking our team captain soon after we arrived what we were going to do the next day. With great enthusiasm he replied, "We're going to knock on the doors of houses throughout the area and tell people about Jesus!"

I swallowed hard and tried to force a positive response. "Oh, boy ..." I said with less than complete enthusiasm, "I hope God uses our efforts!" And then I spent the rest of the evening trying to gear myself up for what promised to be a challenging day ahead.

The following evening at the end of what was, in fact, a pretty hard time for me, I asked what we were going to do the next day. "We're going to go out again, knock on doors, and talk to more people about the Lord!" he said exuberantly.

"Oh ... boy," I muttered.

Day after day we went out trying to find people who were interested, taking every opportunity we could find, doing our best to communicate the good news of Christ to a culture that desperately needed it—but didn't seem to want it.

Some people are made for this kind of direct approach, including door-to-door outreach. It fits their God-given evangelistic style, and they see real results from their efforts. I honor them. I'm just not one of them. For me, this direct, hard-hitting method felt unnatural. I was literally forcing myself, day after day, to do things that seemed to cut across the grain of my personality and temperament.

When the eight weeks were over, I decided *it was really over*. I'd done my time. I'd completed my tour of duty. "Let somebody else sign up for the next campaign," I said to myself. "Evangelism is important, but it's not for me. I'll support it. I'll give to it. I'll pray for it. But don't ask me to go on any more outreach excursions. From here on out, I just want to be an *ordinary* Christian."

## CHURCHES OF "ORDINARY" CHRISTIANS

I don't know how the term *ordinary* ever came to be associated with being uninvolved in evangelism, but it certainly felt natural to me at the time. And, looking around, it seems to feel natural to most Christians. That's why I now believe we're going to have to help them get a new view of what the Bible says should be "ordinary."

I suspect the problem stems from a misconception of what evangelism is and what it can look like in their lives. It's what I've come to refer to as the "problem of perceptions." Even though most Christians have never spent a summer knocking on doors trying to talk to strangers about Jesus, they have similar mental pictures of what they'd have to do if they really became outreach oriented, and they are pretty sure those pictures don't fit them.

In fact, I think most of us tend to have widely polarized images of what evangelism is—mental pictures that are either very positive or very negative. We view it as an activity for superstar Christians who are really good at it. Or, at the other end of the spectrum, we see it as an activity for pushy, out-of-touch individuals who impose themselves and the gospel on everyone they meet. The result of these widely diverse images is that many "ordinary" believers conclude, "I know what evangelism is. It's an activity for superstar Christians who can do it really well—or for people who are just obnoxious enough to do it anyway!" But either way they're convinced it's not for them, because they view themselves as neither extraordinary nor obnoxious!

If we're to ever solve the math problem and enroll the broader church membership in the adventure of relational evangelism, we're going to have to adopt, and then instill into those around us, a new view of what it can look like—one that includes every believer.

It helps that most Christians really do want to make a difference with their lives. Deep down they want to be players on the field and not just spectators in the stands. They want to make investments that will bear fruit and have an impact on eternity. I think the Holy Spirit has inbred these desires in every believer. We just need to show them how they can experience these things—which brings us to Stage 4 of the 6-Stage Process, "TRAIN the Church in Evangelism Skills—the 100 Percent."

And, again, the person whose primary job it is to make sure the entire congregation ends up being exposed to good training is the leader who was empowered back in Stage 3. If we're to have any hope at actually training anywhere near 100 percent of our people, we're going to need a leader to be *focused* on it!

## LIBERATING "ORDINARY" CHRISTIANS

I believe that a primary key to solving the math problem and liberating every Christian in every church to become active in sharing their faith is to help them understand that there are a variety of legitimate approaches to evangelism. In other words, they don't have to squeeze themselves into a specific personality mold in order to be used by God to reach others. In fact, they'll be much more effective if they work within their God-given personality.

Coming back to my own story, this was the discovery that rescued me from the spiritual sidelines. Months after "writing off" evangelism, I went to a midweek worship service at Willow Creek. That night Bill Hybels was speaking on what he called "The Style of an Evangelist." I was tempted to tune him out, presuming that this topic was no longer relevant to me. But as he developed the theme, I began to get more and more interested.

He explained that there are a variety of approaches to evangelism right in the pages of the New Testament. People in the Bible didn't all do outreach the same way, and they didn't pressure each other into doing it the way they did. Reflecting on my recent experiences of feeling out of place doing door-to-door evangelism, I started to perk up quickly.

Bill said he was going to describe six different evangelism styles he'd discovered as he perused the pages of Scripture. The first was the Confrontational Style (we now refer to it as the Direct Style), exemplified by the apostle Peter in Acts 2. Peter was very bold and hard-hitting in the way he communicated the gospel message. He just looked people in the eye and let 'em have it! I thought about how that was more or less what I had tried to do that summer, but how it didn't feel right for me.

Then Bill got to the second example: in Acts 17 the apostle Paul used an Intellectual Style as he stood on Mars Hill in Athens and challenged the philosophers with the claims of Scripture. He presented truth to them in a logical way, and he even quoted some of their own Greek scholars to make his point.

As Bill described this second style I realized my heart was beating quicker! *What an exciting thing*, I thought, *to stand in front of a bunch of skeptics and defend the gospel! I love debating truth with people who aren't yet convinced.* At the time, in fact, I was finishing my master's degree in Philosophy of Religion, but I hadn't fully linked that in my mind with the word *evangelism*. I'd been plagued by the problem of perceptions!

What I realized that night was that my real motivation to read books, to study, and to talk to those with different points of view was to help people move past their intellectual roadblocks and get to the point where they could trust in Christ. I began to understand that I really was made to do evangelism, but in a way that looked different from the approaches

I had tried to use the previous summer. I discovered a new, expanded view of what evangelism is and what it could look like in my life — and in the lives of others.

The Holy Spirit used Bill's words to reorient my thinking and, in effect, to turn the key and unlock the door to my involvement in the area of outreach. And, as a clear manifestation of God's sense of humor, I was hired just a year later to lead the evangelistic charge right there where I heard that message, at Willow Creek Community Church in suburban Chicago, a church that was rapidly becoming known for reaching unchurched people. Since that time, I've had the thrill of developing and utilizing my own intellectual approach to evangelism, both there at that church and many other places. I love talking to and trying to convince spiritual skeptics, on an individual level as well as in larger group settings.

I've also had the privilege of helping many other believers discover and develop their own styles of evangelism through speaking as well as writing (including coauthoring the original and now updated *Becoming a Contagious Christian* book and evangelism training course). I have never found a concept that better liberates Christians who think evangelism is not for them. Whether it be the Direct or Intellectual Styles I've already described, the Testimonial Style of the blind man in John 9, the Interpersonal Style of Matthew in Luke 5:29, the Invitational Style of the Samaritan woman in John 4, or the Serving Style of Tabitha in Acts 9 — or some other biblical approach or combination of approaches — all believers can express their faith in natural ways that will fit their unique personalities.

God built evangelistic diversity into the body of Christ. We need to see that, teach it, live it, and celebrate it as we release believers to communicate Christ in ways that fit them. It takes all kinds of Christians to reach all kinds of non-Christians, and this concept of the six styles of evangelism provides a strategic tool for liberating every believer.[1]

## EVANGELISM TRAINING NEEDED — FOR EVERY BELIEVER

I'm convinced that most pastors greatly overestimate the ability of their members to communicate their faith — in part because they assume that if the church occasionally provides good teaching about it, then folks will be able to go figure out how to do it on their own. But training experts will tell you that most people aren't able to connect the dots in this way. The average person hears and accepts the ideas, and forms good intentions to do something with them, but is at a loss when it comes to actually putting them into action. In between the idea and the action stages, they need an added preparation stage that gives them hands-on opportunities to develop the new skill. This is true in many areas, but especially in the area of evangelism, where so many believers have such low levels of confidence.

That's why evangelism training is needed for *every believer*. Every Christian — regardless of the spiritual gifts he or she may or may not have — is a member of the church to which Jesus gave the Great Commission (Matthew 28:18–20) and consequently has a vital role in fulfilling it. We, as leaders and influencers of our church, need to make sure that they all understand this and do everything in our power to equip them for personal evangelism. This is the only way we're ever going to solve the math problem and become highly contagious churches.

## EFFECTIVE TRAINING IN YOUR CHURCH

The question is, how are we going to accomplish this admittedly ambitious training goal? What steps can we take in our churches to ensure that 100 percent of our members are equipped to communicate their faith to others?

I once thought the answer was first and foremost through providing high-quality training seminars in each church and repeating them regularly until everybody has been equipped. In fact, as the primary author of the *Becoming a Contagious Christian* training course, I originally designed that curriculum around this model — and by God's grace it's had a pretty good measure of impact. Over a decade's time a million people have been trained through the course, in English and in about twenty other languages.

I thank God for how he's used that material, but I no longer think that model is the key to solving the math problem. I think it is part of the key but not the whole of it. In fact, I've learned through teaching this seminar for many years and in many locations that even with the best of efforts, repeated frequently year after year, most churches end up only training about 10–20 percent of their members. That's because the seminar model is an incremental approach that relies on believers becoming motivated enough to take a day or a series of evenings out of their busy schedules to come and learn about something that, on the face of it, already scares and in many cases repels them! Thankfully some of them still show up—but the majority don't. We won't ever get to 100 percent of the church in that way.

It was after fighting uphill battles for a long time trying to train entire churches in this fashion that I finally had a "Copernican Revolution": I realized that we needed to stop relying solely on a plan to get church members to revolve around our training agenda by signing up and coming to us for a seminar. Rather, we need to start revolving around them by taking the training to places they're already showing up—namely, weekend services, small groups, and in some churches, adult Sunday school classes (as well as still offering elective seminars as a supplement).

It was this "revolution" in my thinking, along with observing the impact of various churchwide campaigns that were being used, especially Rick Warren's "40 Days of Purpose," which led to a more complete idea: Why not focus entire churches all at once for a campaign on what is arguably their central purpose here on earth—reaching lost people?

Thus was born the vision for churchwide *Contagious Campaigns*. Churches could, over a six-week period, utilize Sunday sermons to inform and inspire their congregations *and* sync up all their small groups and classes throughout the church to do the updated training course (a *Youth Edition*[2] is available for junior high and high school student ministries). In this way, everyone gets on the same page, learning their various evangelism styles and the basics of sharing their faith with others.

The timing of this vision coincided with the work I was just beginning of updating and revising the *Becoming a Contagious Christian* training course in partnership with the Willow Creek Association (www.willowcreek.com) and Zondervan (www.zondervan.com). The end result was an updated course that can serve better than ever as a stand-alone seminar (with a facilitator from the church using the new *Leader's Guide* and *PowerPoint*)—which is a great way to introduce the training to the church as well as to offer a supplement to the small group and Sunday school options in the *Contagious Campaign*. Seminars are also great ways to provide follow-up training after a *Contagious Campaign*, to train newcomers and sharpen the skills of members who need a refresher.

But more than being just an updated seminar, the new materials also include six sermon transcripts for the Sunday services (on the CD-ROM; messages to be modified as needed) as well as a set of training DVDs of Lee Strobel and me teaching the entire course, so small group and class leaders can use a simple "plug-and-play" approach and let us teach the materials for them!

What's more, the *Contagious Campaign* culminates with a final sixth-week message designed to actually present the gospel to all the friends that church members will invite. So this is not merely training and preparation for believers; it's also a chance to apply what is being learned, invite neighbors, and see a harvest of people trusting in Christ on the final week.

In addition, Outreach, Inc. has provided an array of high-quality publicity and communication tools to help give your churchwide *Contagious Campaign* visibility and maximize its impact (see: www.outreach.com or www.contagiouschristian.com). Outreach also has partnered to provide a group of seasoned speakers, any of whom could come to your church to supplement your team and teach at one of the Sunday services during a *Contagious Campaign*, or to do a classic one-day training seminar (see: www.outreachspeakers.com).

It is my heartfelt hope that these new materials in the updated *Contagious* course and *Contagious Campaign* serve you and your church in training all of your members to communicate their faith in natural ways, as well as to actually reach many of their friends, family members, neighbors, and coworkers for Christ.

## KEY EVANGELISM TRAINING ELEMENTS

We've talked in a general way about the kind of evangelism training I'd recommend, but now let's briefly discuss the key components in the training we designed specifically to fill this purpose: the updated and revised *Becoming a Contagious Christian* curriculum. This is one of several courses available, but it is the only one I know of that liberates believers by showing them how they can discover and develop their own natural style. This helps the majority of church members who are skeptical about evangelism to stay engaged long enough to catch the vision and start developing new skills.

The course will also help your church members:

■ **Get a new view of evangelism**

The first thing we do in the *Contagious* course is try to displace the limiting stereotypes, both positive and negative, and replace them with a positive image of what evangelism can look like in our lives.

■ **Pray for God's involvement**

Evangelism is God's idea, and without him we're powerless to have a spiritual impact on others. Therefore we don't end the first session without praying together for the people we hope to reach and wisdom on how to do so.

■ **Find your own style**

Through teaching and a "Styles Questionnaire," we help every participant discover which of the six biblical evangelism styles—or combination of styles—fits them. This is both freeing and encouraging.

■ **Build and deepen relationships**

This one is pivotal: most Christians have very few non-Christian friends. We address this problem by giving ideas and encouragement for deepening relationships with the people participants already know, reigniting relationships with people they used to know, and beginning new relationships with people they'd like to know.

■ **Start spiritual conversations**

Some Christians break out of their safety zones and build relationships with unbelievers but never say anything about their faith. This prevents them from becoming contagious carriers of the gospel. Therefore we teach, watch true-to-life drama vignettes on DVD, and then try several practical approaches to raising spiritual topics. This is a real confidence builder.

■ **Tell their stories**

One of your most powerful tools for reaching others is the account of how God reached you. Following Paul's example in Acts 26, we use six questions to flesh out our own stories, building them around a simple, easy-to-remember outline that participants can use to tell their stories clearly and concisely. They also watch an effective example on a drama DVD and then give it a try themselves. This role-playing practice component is a very important part of the training—as important as the experience of learning in a flight simulator is to an airplane pilot! We learn first in a safe environment, so we're confident and ready when there's a real opportunity!

■ **Communicate God's message**

The most important part of evangelism training is teaching people to convey the central message of the Christian faith. We do this through several "how-to-share" illustrations, DVD drama vignettes, and practice time. The gospel truly is "the power of God for the salvation of everyone who believes" (Romans 1:16). We just have to put it into the hands of all of our church's members, challenge them to take some risks to communicate it to others, and let God show his power through it.

■ **Help friends cross the line of faith**

Many believers are tempted to bail out of the action and call in a "professional" when the time comes to lead another person across the line of faith. But this is the most exciting part, so why not experience it? Thus, we teach participants how they can lead their friends in a natural, conversational prayer in which they prompt their friends to ask Christ, in their own words, for his forgiveness and leadership. We follow this with a powerful drama on DVD, which both teaches and inspires them to do the same.

■ **Ensure next steps**

The final part of the process is following up with those who have put their trust in Christ. We teach participants to help new believers form healthy relationships with other Christians in a biblically functioning church and to encourage them to establish regular patterns of prayer, Bible study, and worship that will enhance their spiritual growth.

From my experience, as well as from the letters and emails I receive from all around the world, it's clear that this training builds confidence and gives participants a sense that this is something they really can do—because they've just tried it in a safe training environment! As you train people in your church, I'm confident that stories will multiply. Courage will grow. Faith will expand. Seekers will meet Christ, and the presence of these new believers will motivate more and more believers to get into the action. Things will get *contagious*—inside the church first, and then increasingly outside the church!

## TEN TIPS FOR EFFECTIVE EVANGELISM TRAINING SEMINARS

For those times when you do training using the classic seminar model, here are some suggestions to help have a maximum impact (some of these especially pertain to the *Becoming a Contagious Christian* course, but the principles are easily transferable):

1. *When you're introducing the training, follow the three-part rule: communicate, communicate, and communicate.* Putting an invitation in the bulletin and having someone read it as part of the announcements is not enough. Evangelism training needs to be highlighted, explained, and promoted—especially by the senior pastor. This message can be reinforced with mailings, emails, flyers, and posters.

    A bulletin announcement might look something like this:

---

### BECOME A DIFFERENCE MAKER!

God wants to use you to impact the spiritual lives of your friends and family. Join us on Saturday, May 8, for the *Becoming a Contagious Christian* training, where you'll learn to naturally and effectively communicate your faith to people you know (this course is especially for people who don't like evangelism). It's an adventure you won't want to miss! Stop by the *Contagious* booth after the service to find out more or to sign up.

---

2. *Ask people who are planning to attend to sign up ahead of time* (and make it easy for them to do so through multiple paths: email, voice mail, a booth after services, and so forth). This will help you plan for room size (get a room that is just barely big enough—it's better to be crowded in a bit), refreshments, and the right number of Participant's Guides and any other handouts. Be sure to allow for a few walk-ins too. Also, consider setting a moderate fee or "suggested donation" to help cover the cost of materials and refreshments. Most people don't mind investing a little in something they consider important.

3. *Keep a record of who attends in case you want to get back to them about other training or outreach opportunities.* Also, I'd suggest using the "Styles Survey" in the Leader's Guide to collect information on participants' top evangelism style or styles; this will help you know whom to contact for what kind of event!

4. *Book the best quality room you can get, set it up in advance, and make sure it is as clean and organized as it possibly can be.* This is one of the church's most strategic events, so treat it as such. (The banners, posters, and other materials available at Outreach, Inc. can help give your seminar a professional look.)

5. *Depending on the size of the group, you may need a sound system as well as lights focused on the trainer.* If so, be sure to use a lapel or headset microphone so you can be mobile, and make sure it is tested and ready well before people arrive. Do the same with the DVD player and PowerPoint projector.

6. *Recruit the friendliest and most winsome volunteers you can find to greet people, distribute materials, and serve refreshments.* Make sure they go through the training themselves so they'll be able to talk enthusiastically about the course and the impact it has had on their own outreach efforts.

7. *Play upbeat instrumental music as people arrive, with the volume a little higher than typical background music.* People need to see— and feel—that this will not be a formal church service but an exciting gathering of friendly people.

8. *Start and end on time.* Even though the sessions can be done in about an hour each, I'd recommend allowing, if possible, some extra time for questions and storytelling.

9. *If you're teaching the course live using the Leader's Guide (as opposed to the DVDs of Lee Strobel and me teaching it), make sure that you are thoroughly familiar with the materials and prepared to lead.* This will help you to not be too tied to the Leader's Guide or worried about when to show drama DVDs or switch PowerPoint screens. Every time you teach the course you'll feel more relaxed and it will become more fun. Soon the biggest challenge will be to stay within the time frames, because you'll be gaining more and more stories and illustrations you'll want to tell!

10. *Be sure to announce to the group, both verbally and by means of a printed flyer, when the next offering of training will be.* Especially at the last session, you need to commission these freshly fired-up evangelists to go out and be your ambassadors in encouraging others in the church to come to the course. These people will be the best promoters; put them to work! Also let them know that, as alumni, they're always welcome to come back for a refresher whenever the course is taught.

## THE IMPACT OF EVANGELISTIC TRAINING

I could tell a lot of stories about people and churches that have put evangelism training to work. Some are on a large scale, like the church in Georgia that taught nearly a thousand people all at once through their Sunday school classes. Others are unexpected, like the church in Iowa, where a seminar participant who had been spiritually sitting on the fence decided to trust Christ and prayed right there in the middle of the class! Some are heartwarming, like the woman at our church who led both of her aging parents to faith, or the junior high boy who used his toy building blocks to show his grandmother a gospel illustration and ended up leading her in a prayer of commitment. Others are humorous, like the woman who took a coworker to lunch the day after the session on how to explain the gospel. She told her friend what she'd learned, presented the plan of salvation, and ended up praying with her in the car as they drove back to work—while the friend was driving!

Do you see what's happening? It's the replacement of the old 1 x 100 approach with the much more powerful 100 x 1. Instead of one "professional" trying to lead everybody to Christ, more and more ordinary Christians are getting in the game, and the impact is expanding exponentially. It's a reversal of the ratios—and an important step toward solving the math problem we discussed at the beginning of the chapter.

I conclude this chapter with an account that poignantly illustrates the power of training people to share Christ. The story was told in a letter from Todd, a church leader in Ontario, Canada, who had just returned home from an evangelism conference I'd hosted and helped teach. After a brief introduction, he wrote this:

> Currently we are teaching the *Becoming a Contagious Christian* material on Sunday evenings. Keith, the newly appointed coordinator of our Strategic Evangelism Ministry, and I were teaching session 5 of the curriculum, the one about presenting the gospel message, this past Sunday night. As you know, this is the session that presents the Bridge illustration.
>
> I laid out the theology portion, and then Keith taught through the drawing. As he explained each component, we had people reproduce the drawing on napkins he'd handed out in order to simulate a real-life scenario! Many children were there for the service, and they drew the picture too. At least one ten-year-old boy, Matthew, decided to accept Jesus after drawing the picture and discussing it with his father.

But I want to tell you about my own son, Joel, who is six years old and quite a little "intellectual." Up until this weekend he had no interest in talking to us about spiritual things. Perhaps he was a bit of a junior skeptic! But Sunday was different. In his class that morning, Keith had encouraged the children to pray to receive Christ, and we found out later that Joel had done so.

Then, Sunday evening during the service, Joel, like the other children present, drew the Bridge drawing. When my wife later asked him where he could be found on the drawing, he said, "I prayed with Pastor Keith this morning, and I think I'm over here with God."

Needless to say, we were very excited! His hesitancy to talk about spiritual things was lifted, and we enjoyed a fantastic conversation in the van on the way home.

But then, as soon as we drove into the driveway, Joel jumped out and announced that he was going to show his napkin to Agnes, our next-door neighbor we've been trying to reach out to! He ran to her door and explained his Bridge drawing in detail!

Then he asked her, "Where are you on the drawing?" She placed herself one step onto the Bridge. He then proceeded to invite her to our church, and she accepted without hesitation.

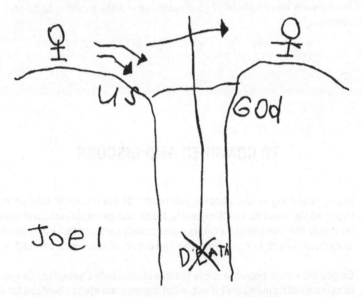

The work of Joel, an evangelistically liberated and equipped six-year-old.

> This little boy accepted Christ in the morning, learned the Bridge illustration in the evening, and within a half hour of the service had used it to explain the gospel to an unchurched person! What an incredible answer to the prayers I've been praying since Joel came into the world six years ago.

If Joel, a six-year-old boy who had just met Christ, can be used in this way, then so can you, me, and all of the other Christians in our churches! But that kind of action won't happen in most of our members' lives without an intentional evangelism training program to equip and encourage them.

Becoming a contagious church that reaches the unchurched community largely depends on that kind of training. The task is too huge to be done on the backs of a few pastors, church leaders, or evangelism enthusiasts. We need nothing less than the unleashing of the entire body of Christ—*every* member of *every* church being trained and deployed to communicate his or her faith with confidence.

**STAGE 4: KEY IDEA**

*Your church must train all of your members—100 percent—to be contagious.*

> Everyone who is fully trained will be like his teacher. (Luke 6:40)

# TO CONSIDER AND DISCUSS

1. In the beginning of this chapter you read: "Of the churches that do train their people, most do so infrequently, teach just one approach, and have a relatively low number of members who actually participate." How does this statement reflect, or not reflect, the current situation in your church?

2. Do you think your church is ready to run a churchwide *Contagious Campaign* to equip all of its members? If not, what incremental steps could you take to get there?

3. When it comes to evangelism, what do you think an "ordinary" follower of Christ should look like?

4. What are some practical and creative ways you can promote evangelism training in your church?

5. If you've been through an evangelism training program, how has it influenced your effectiveness as a witness for Jesus Christ? How might you be helped by a refresher course?

# CHAPTER SIX

# STAGE 5: MOBILIZE THE CHURCH'S EVANGELISM SPECIALISTS—THE 10 PERCENT

IMAGINE THAT A WEALTHY PERSON in your town decides to promote better fitness by setting up a citywide basketball tournament. He announces that any organization, including schools, civic clubs, neighborhood groups—and yes, churches, too—can put together a team to compete. Then to get people motivated, he declares that he'll give the winning team a million dollars, to go to the charity or nonprofit organization of their choice. Now, do you suppose your church might be interested in putting together a team? A cool million sure would help with that upcoming capital fund drive, don't you think?

Assuming you agree, you would need to get busy right away putting together your church's team. As you started looking around at the people in your congregation, you'd discover that lots of your members can more-or-less play basketball. In other words, they're able to dribble the ball, toss it to teammates, and fling it in the general direction of the hoop. So you could just recruit a few readily available people from your congregation, talk them into playing, and in a sense you'd have "a team."

But before you selected your final roster, wouldn't it be nice to find out that there are a couple of former standout college players and a recently retired NBA star who have been hovering around the fringes of your church? I think you'll agree that this would be helpful information before finally deciding who will make the cut, form the team, and represent you and your church to compete for the big prize!

In this chapter we're talking about a subject much more important than any basketball game or monetary reward. We're talking about putting together a group of evangelists who can spiritually impact the lives of people all around your community—not just for today, but for all of eternity!

And you know what? You've got something that goes well beyond the natural abilities—incredible as they are—of even an NBA player. You've got people in your congregation who have been given a divine enablement from God, called the spiritual gift of evangelism, to help them reach lots of people for Christ. And it would be as crazy to try to become a contagious church while ignoring these gifted evangelists as it would be to build your basketball team while ignoring the basketball stars sitting in the wings.

Yet that's exactly what George Barna discovered many of us to be doing! He reports in his book *Evangelism That Works* that when he studied the practices of many churches he found that they "paraded new converts before the congregation to encourage the entire body." But they did this "without mentioning that the converts' decision to embrace Christ had been facilitated through the diligent and obedient efforts of a particular person or group of people. The attention of the church body was trained exclusively upon the evangelized, *ignoring the role and model of the evangelizers.*"[1]

## AVOIDING COMMON PITFALLS

That's a pretty good description of the first of two extremes churches fall into related to their gifted evangelists: they simply leave them alone. At best, this approach says, "We know they're out there in the congregation somewhere—God bless 'em—and we sure hope they're doing their job!"

But we need to find these people so we can acknowledge and encourage and build into them—particularly because they face the kinds of obstacles we've discussed earlier, such as evangelistic entropy, the problem of perceptions, and the ongoing efforts of the Evil One to keep them spiritually sidetracked. We need to call these people out of isolation and begin to develop them.

We also need to avoid the second extreme some churches fall into, which is to keep them together all of the time. This is a danger inherent in starting a traditional "evangelism team." Outreach-oriented members can end up moving from their original situation of being isolated *from* each another to, all of a sudden, becoming isolated *with* each another. As a result, they're now hanging out with a bunch of outreach types most of the time and no longer participating in or influencing the rest of the areas of the church.

As Becky Pippert reminded us in her classic book *Out of the Saltshaker and Into the World*, salt has to be scattered before it does any good. "Salty" people not only need to be spread throughout the neighborhoods, they also need to be spread throughout the church's ministries. Think about it. If we really want to build a contagious, outwardly focused church, are there any ministries that don't need at least a few evangelism enthusiasts in their midst? I can't think of any!

We need these people among the greeters and ushers who have direct contact with people who visit our services. We need them with the children, the students, the singles, the couples, the men's ministry, and the women's ministry. We need them on the hospital visitation teams, at the food pantry, in the homeless ministry, on the missions board as well as on the mission field, in the small group ministry, on the Sunday school teaching team, and certainly mixed in with the elder and deacon boards. We need their catalytic, contagious influence everywhere!

To build off of Paul's "fan into flame" metaphor in 2 Timothy 1:6, every evangelist in the church (using that term "evangelist" broadly to include anyone with gifts or passion in the area of evangelism, regardless of which of the six evangelism styles he or she might have) is like a burning ember in a bonfire. If we leave those embers out on their own, isolated somewhere in the church, they will lose their intensity and grow cold. On the other hand, if we go to the other extreme and keep them together in one place, they'll burn bright and hot, but they'll have almost no effect on the environment outside of their immediate circle. So we can't leave them alone, to be sure, but neither can we pull them completely away into an evangelism team that is separate from the other ministries.

See the problem? I spent long hours trying to find a workable solution to this conundrum—one that would allow us to find and build into the evangelists in the church, yet keep them strategically spread throughout the ministries of the church. What I finally figured out with the help of a couple of other leaders was that we needed to develop *a new kind of evangelism ministry*. It would be a centralized, cross-departmental, multistyled, easy-access, regular-but-not-too-frequent gathering of evangelism enthusiasts from all over the church. In the terms of our 6-Stage Process, we needed to move into Stage 5, which is to: "MOBILIZE the Church's Evangelism Specialists—the 10 percent."

## THE SHAPE OF THIS MINISTRY

This new ministry would provide a place where evangelists could come for inspiration and ideas, but not a place where they would set up permanent residence. Our goal is to bring them in, build them up, and send them back out. Thus, it becomes a *team* only in a loose sense. In reality it is a gathering of all of the ministries' evangelism leaders and teams, organized and led by the church's evangelism leader. This evangelism ministry is *centralized* and *cross-departmental*, because evangelism is a value and activity that transcends any one ministry or group of people. Our purpose is to become a contagious *church*, not just a contagious department or two.

The evangelism team is *multistyled*, because we believe in a wide range of evangelistic approaches. We're convinced it really does take all kinds of Christians to reach all kinds of non-Christians. So it is crucial that the team not be dominated by one style or one ministry emphasis that pushes everyone else to conform. Rather, it embraces and celebrates evangelistic diversity and then builds on it.

The meetings need to be *easy access* in the sense that we try to remove all unnecessary barriers to attendance (evangelism has enough barriers of its own!). This means picking a convenient time, choosing a central location, keeping any registration processes simple, holding costs for food or any materials to a minimum (sometimes completely subsidizing these costs), and making it clear that there are no other implied commitments that come with showing up. It also means assuring potential attendees that they don't need a lot of outreach experience or confidence in their evangelistic abilities to be part of the group. We avoid projecting the idea that this is an elite corps of specialists. We tell folks that if they have a passion in this area, or if they'd like to develop more passion for it, they ought to give one of these gatherings a try.

These team meetings are frequent enough to build some relationships and momentum but *not too frequent*. Too many meetings force people to choose between this ministry and the other areas in the church where they're already involved. Therefore I'd recommend holding these gatherings about four to six times a year. The inner core of evangelists will likely want more, and you can give those folks other next-step opportunities, including leadership roles. But this limited number of meetings enables a broader group of people from the other ministries to become active with the ministry.

Another advantage to offering meetings less often is that it enables better planning and an investment in higher quality elements, whether guest speakers, music, media presentations, or printed materials. This is necessary to help busy people stay motivated to participate on an ongoing basis.

Generally I'd avoid meeting immediately before or after weekend services, because these are often good places to bring friends, and we want members to be free to attend the services with them. In other words, don't ask them to attend outreach ministry meetings when you really want them to be *doing* outreach! I've found that Saturday morning breakfast meetings work well, including time for eating, interacting at the tables, a short break, and then the main program.

## GIVING THE MINISTRY A NAME

When we started this ministry at Willow Creek, we didn't want to call it the "Evangelism Team" because of the stereotypes conjured up by such a name. After considering many options, we finally decided to call it the Frontline ministry because its participants really are on the front lines of the action!

Since then many other churches have recognized the need to begin similar ministries, and some of them have also used the name Frontline, as well as names like Reach, Ignite, and others. I welcome this trend and hope this book will help more churches, yours included, learn how to begin their own gatherings to inspire and mobilize their own outreach enthusiasts.

## COMPONENTS OF FRONTLINE MEETINGS

Following are some of the main elements I've found to be important in Frontline-type gatherings with the evangelism specialists in churches. Depending on the priorities of the particular meeting, these will vary in order and degree of emphasis. As you move into Stage 5 and begin to plan these kinds of gatherings, you'll be able to determine what is appropriate each time, based on prayer and a general consensus between your evangelism leader and the other leaders in the evangelism ministry.

## Strategic Leadership

You're becoming a church with clear evangelistic vision. But apart from organizing a regular gathering—along the lines of a Frontline ministry—when do you ever have the chance to speak to the evangelistically gifted and impassioned core of your church? Apart from something like this, you're left, at best, with a shotgun approach that tries to encourage and mobilize the evangelists at the same time that the whole church is gathered. But this approach provides the forum for strategic evangelistic leadership.

## Relational Connections

One constant in these meetings is the opportunity for these people to connect with other like-minded outreach enthusiasts. If all we did was get these people together in a room and turn them loose to talk to each other about their evangelistic efforts, we'd be serving an important need! It's the "logs in a bonfire" effect. The key is to schedule plenty of time for this, and resist the temptation to fill the entire time with teaching and activities.

That's why having a meal together works so well. It gives folks relaxed time to talk. Also, you can seed the conversations by giving them questions to discuss that relate to some aspect of evangelism you're going to address later in the meeting.

It's easy to underestimate how important this connection time is. Evangelism can be a very lonely endeavor. Discouragement and feelings of inadequacy can easily set in. This is why we need to facilitate discussions that help members realize that such feelings are common and that allow them to encourage each other.

## Stimulating Stories

The strongest tool for encouraging evangelists is sharing stories about how God is working in our midst. Since nothing has a more powerful effect, I make this the heart of these meetings, giving it more priority than teaching or vision casting.

When I started writing this chapter I received an email message from Jim, a member of the Frontline ministry, telling me that at a "Matthew Party" he recently sponsored, eight people made first-time commitments to Christ. (A Matthew Party is what we call social events designed to mix believers with unbelievers in a safe social setting. We derived the name from Jesus' disciple, Matthew, who held such an event in Luke 5:29.) A few days later I received a note from another friend who had written out his testimony, explaining what had convinced him to become a Christian. He told me about a letter he had received from an atheist who had recently read his story and trusted in Christ. I was not directly involved with either of these situations but, needless to say, the news greatly encouraged and motivated me—and I knew it would have a similar effect on the Frontline members.

I like to facilitate the sharing of stories like these in several different ways. One approach is to have one of the leaders encourage those at the gathering who have an exciting story (or a difficult experience they've learned from) to tell the rest of the group. Opening up the floor for anyone to share a story has its risks, and occasionally a leader needs to step in and help the person speaking get back on track. But some of the most inspiring and joy-filled stories have emerged in this way.

Another approach is to ask a team member ahead of time to be prepared to tell the group about how God has worked through him or her. Many times one of us will informally interview the person with the story. That gives us the chance to clarify facts, correct any misunderstandings, interject a bit of humor, and occasionally drive home an important point. This format also tends to put the one telling the story at ease.

I remember interviewing a man named Bob at one of the first Frontline meetings I ever led. Bob had taken some evangelistic risks in a conversation with a friend a couple of weeks earlier. In animated tones he told us how inadequate and nervous he felt going into the situation. In fact, he said his hands had been shaking so badly that he literally had to sit on them while he shared the gospel with his friend! Nevertheless, before the conversation was finished, he led his friend in a prayer of commitment to Christ!

As Bob told his story he could barely force himself to stay seated on the stool next to me. You can imagine the excitement this evoked in all of the evangelism enthusiasts who listened. They were all saying to themselves, "Wow, I want more of that kind of action in my life! I could take the kinds of steps Bob took—my hands don't even shake as much as his did! Surely God can use me in that way too." They walked out at the end of the meeting much more motivated to take risks for the sake of the gospel.

Look for success stories you can highlight within your group. These stories will encourage and challenge the team as nothing else will. In addition, you can choose the best stories and use them in your worship services—with either you or another leader telling them (with the person's explicit permission), or the persons telling the stories themselves. This will honor those folks for their evangelistic service, and further instill these values throughout the congregation.

## Teaching, Inspiration, and Skills Reinforcement

Teaching can be another important component of the Frontline gathering, although I don't view these meetings as classes or as duplicates of the *Becoming a Contagious Christian* course. Rather, we remind members that if they haven't been through "basic training" yet, they ought to go through the course as soon as possible, whether in a seminar or in their class or small group.

Frontline meetings are, however, a great place to expose your core evangelists to teachers from inside and outside the church. I look for speakers who can encourage them in their efforts, inspire them to express their God-given evangelistic potential, and challenge them to make the most of every opportunity. Sometimes I've also expanded on the broad themes of the *Contagious* training and given new ideas and examples that members can add to their evangelistic skill-sets. For example, we've taught fresh illustrations of the gospel message—or even reviewed old ones—and had people pair up and practice them.

At one particular meeting we felt we needed to reinforce the importance of all of us being ready to help people make decisions for Christ. Many team members were doing pretty well at encouraging friends in their spiritual journeys, but not at assisting these friends in actually putting their trust in Christ. So we designed a Frontline meeting around the theme of "Crossing the Line of Faith."

First, we talked about the soccer metaphor of "putting the ball in the net." Then I role-played with a friend named Dan, who had recently come to Christ. He was fresh enough in the faith that I knew he wouldn't use a lot of religious clichés. Our short "drama" seemed to go well, and later many in the group told us they found it helpful. We ended the meeting in prayer, asking God for opportunities and for boldness to apply what we'd learned.

Two days later I got a call from Jim, one of our key members, who told me that he'd already applied the lessons during a flight on a business trip. He said, "Mark, normally I would have simply presented the gospel, encouraged the man to consider what I'd said, assured him that I'd be praying for him, and then dropped the subject. But after what I learned on Saturday morning, I decided to take a risk and ask him if he would like to receive the forgiveness and leadership of Christ. Much to my surprise, he was ready! We prayed together right there on the plane, and today we have a new brother in Christ." When you see results like this, it's easy to stay motivated in planning quality Frontline events!

Below are a few other examples of topics you may want to address in your meetings, although in some cases you may not want to announce the topic until the team arrives. Build excitement around the gathering itself, with its relationships and fresh doses of encouragement, rather than around the specific topic or speaker.

- Praying for lost friends and family
- Leading small groups for spiritual seekers
- Designing creative Matthew Parties
- Building confidence in the reliability of the Bible
- Answering your skeptic friend's toughest challenges
- Pointing to the evidence for creation over evolution
- Reaching your Jewish friend for Jesus
- Understanding and interacting with Muslim teachings
- Mastering the gospel message
- Exploring new arenas for redemptive relationships
- Finding fresh ways to start spiritual conversations
- Taking steps to develop your evangelistic style
- Finding courage to take spiritual risks
- Dealing with discouragement in personal evangelism

Depending on the size of your Frontline ministry and the resources available, you may want to consider adding other elements to your meetings, such as music, short movie or video clips, dramas, worship segments, or multimedia presentations. But only add what fits the theme, what can be done with excellence, and what will relate to the group.

Never add elements just for the sake of having more elements. You'd be better off expanding the storytelling or teaching time.

## Guest Speakers

Outside speakers can be an important addition — or a detriment, depending on whom you bring. You have a limited number of opportunities to encourage this team, so choose meeting elements and teachers carefully. A guest speaker may be well known and powerful in other arenas, but not necessarily fit your Frontline ministry. Search for the right teachers who will understand and relate to the unique challenges of reaching others for Christ.

Where can you find good speakers? Some may already be in the Frontline group or in your church. Others may be in different churches in your town or region. Perhaps you know a leader in your denomination that would fit the bill (but don't assume someone will fit just because that person has "Evangelism" in his or her title). Another possibility is a Christian professor at a college or seminary in the area. I've tried to keep my eyes open for opportunities to piggyback on other events happening in the region. Perhaps an evangelistic teacher or writer is coming to speak for a conference or outreach event. Maybe he or she would enjoy spending an hour encouraging a team of budding evangelists. Remember, don't say no for the person without letting him or her have the chance to say yes! Also, especially when you're first starting out, don't overlook the option of using effective talks on video.

My general rule for inviting guest speakers is that I need to first hear them speak, at a minimum, on CD or video. I once asked an out-of-town speaker I was thinking about inviting to send me a video of his teaching. "What is this, an audition?" he chided. "Well, yeah, I guess it sort of is," I said, quickly adding, "I just want to make sure it'll be a good fit ... so when can you send me a video?" He sent one, we invited him to speak, he served us well, and we're still friends today!

This may feel a bit awkward, but it's far better than sitting through an agonizing hour listening while the wrong person squanders the opportunity to build into this important group of outreach advocates. Also, after hearing a recording of a potential speaker, you may be able to coach him or her to better fit your group's needs.

Whatever you do in terms of teaching, keep the standard high and make sure it speaks directly to the needs of your team members.

## Inside Scoop on Upcoming Opportunities

One of the most strategic aspects of having your key evangelists together is the opportunity to highlight upcoming evangelism training or outreach events. In some situations, you'll want them to attend for their own development. At other times, you'll want them to have the inside track on an event so they'll know how to invite their non-Christian friends. Or you might be looking for them to get involved in making the event happen, from planning to promotion to execution. Frontline meetings provide a pool of prequalified candidates for a whole range of strategic initiatives. Let members have a share of the action. They'll thank you for giving them an important role to play.

## Highlight Redemptive Resources

One of the things I enjoy most is introducing high-quality outreach tools to people who will actually use them. Almost all of the books and magazines in Christian bookstores are designed for Christians, but once in a while you come across a resource that was published with spiritual seekers in mind. When you find one, be sure to tell the group about it! Better yet, give them samples at your meeting and help them think through how they can use them. At our meetings we've also given out copies of *Outreach* magazine,[2] a great publication filled with ideas and inspiration for every outreach-minded Christian.

We also highlight valuable seeker-oriented resources, such as:

- *The Journey: A Bible for the Spiritually Curious*, an NIV reference Bible designed specifically for spiritual seekers and new believers[3]
- *The Case for Christ, The Case for Faith, The Case for a Creator*, and *The Case for the Real Jesus* by Lee Strobel[4]
- *More Than a Carpenter* by Josh McDowell[5]
- *The Reason Why* by Robert Laidlaw[6]
- *Tough Questions*, a proven curriculum for seeker small groups, by Garry Poole and Judson Poling[7]

These kinds of resources are not just great tools for the team to have available to give to people after they've started talking to them; they are actually catalysts to help them start talking to people about spiritual matters in the first place. I was on an airplane, for example, and just as we were about to land, I struck up a conversation with a woman sitting next to me. As we talked, I remembered I had an excerpt from *The Journey* Bible in my briefcase. Just knowing I had it gave me the confidence to move this friendly little exchange in a more significant direction by saying, "By the way, I have something here I think you might enjoy reading. I'd like to give it to you." She seemed to appreciate it, and it led us into a conversation about spiritual matters. I'm pretty sure this wouldn't have happened if I hadn't had that resource in my briefcase. The key is to help all of our Frontline members keep appropriate outreach tools in their briefcases, purses, backpacks, desk drawers, and glove compartments. It's a tangible way to help them "be prepared to give an answer to everyone who asks" (1 Peter 3:15).

## United Prayer

Frontline meetings are also good places to remind people—and give them an opportunity—to pray for their lost friends. Prayer is usually just a segment of a broader meeting program, but occasionally it's good to make it the whole theme, with teaching on prayer, encouragement to keep praying, and extended time for members to pray together for their non-Christian friends.

You might want to also start a dedicated prayer team within this ministry (or connect with the church's broader prayer team). It can collect requests at meetings and in between gatherings through emails or phone calls, and in a dedicated and consistent way bring to God the needs and requests of the evangelism activists in your church. When we pray along these lines, God seems to delight in answering our prayers!

## Healthy Accountability

A natural outflow of the group interactions is an increased level of accountability. Sometimes just knowing that someone else in the ministry might ask us about our evangelistic efforts can prompt us to do more of the right things to reach out to others for Christ. While we might wish we were always moved to action by loftier motivations, the end result is still what we want to have happen in and through our lives.

Accountability may also be increased by forming small groups out of the larger gatherings. These groups enable ongoing communication and encouragement to stay active in praying for and reaching out to those we hope to influence.

There is a fine line to walk, however, in this area of accountability. People often already feel excessive guilt and inadequacy about evangelism, so we must be careful not to harshly challenge or shame them. If we do, they'll just feel worse and will likely start avoiding us rather than moving toward increased prayer and activity to reach others. Direct challenges have their place, but it's usually best to stick with encouragement and gentle reminders.

## Appreciation and Thanks

Unfortunately, as we mentioned earlier in this chapter, the people in the church who are most gifted by the Holy Spirit to fulfill the Great Commission are often some of the most neglected by the church. This is extremely counterproductive. Evangelism can be a difficult, isolated activity, and the people engaged in it need lots of encouragement and affirmation, especially from the church's leaders. Frontline meetings are a great place to do this, and they help you identify those you might also want to recognize and thank in front of the entire church as well.

These folks are pacesetters. By their words and actions they call everyone in the church to take risks for the sake of the gospel. In the spiritual battle for souls, we need to highlight and encourage all of these heroes we can find, and let their actions inspire the entire congregation.

## FINDING THE CHURCH'S EVANGELISTIC CORE

You may be thinking, *Yes, but where do you find these people? As you said earlier, they don't just stand up and identify themselves!*

### The "Bubble Up" Approach

We can and must find them. Stage 4 (training the church) causes the 10 percent of church members with gifts and passion for evangelism to surface in ways the other stages don't. The first three stages—living evangelistic lives, instilling evangelistic values, and empowering an evangelism leader—are the prerequisites that help make it possible to get these people into a training situation that can draw out their evangelism gift. And even after all of that, they'll often come hesitantly. That's okay. If you can just get everyone involved in evangelism training, they'll all benefit, they'll all find their natural style and gain skills in communicating their faith, and those with the gift will tend to bubble to the surface.

My friend Karl Singer came up with a great description of this. He said, "What you're doing is throwing everybody into the water and teaching them all to swim. But then you're watching for those who really take to it—the natural swimmers—and then putting them on your champion swimming team."

Karl's right. Every church has at least a few of these potential champions, but you have to look for them, enroll them, and develop them.

## Use Training Campaigns and Seminars

As you teach people in the church to communicate their faith, whether in seminars or a *Contagious Campaign*, you'll see these potential specialists start to come alive. They inch toward the edge of their chairs, listen intently, and jot down a lot of notes. During breaks and after sessions (and sometimes during sessions) they can't wait to talk to you, ask questions, and tell stories. They're the ones who, at the end of the final session, come up and ask why the course has to be so short. *These are the right people!*

In the *Becoming a Contagious Christian* book we talked about a man named Fred who was coaxed by a church staff member to go through the training course. Fred's initial reaction was to scoff. "I'm no evangelist," he assured the staff member. But he ended up coming to the training, even if under a bit of duress. And over the next several weeks I could see him coming to life. In fact, he'd never let me get a break during the break times! Like putting a match to lighter fluid, this man was ignited. This was the beginning of an ongoing friendship with Fred, including many discussions on the phone and in person when he'd ask me, as his "coach," for advice on various witnessing opportunities.

The Frontline ministry was a natural next step for Fred. In the years that followed, he led more people to Christ than we could keep track of. But Fred never would have shown up if we had simply announced, "Everyone with the gift of evangelism please meet this Saturday morning." We had to go after him—and this has been true of many others who later become part of the Frontline group.

## Look with Purpose

When you notice these kinds of people, seize the moment. Pull them aside and tell them you can see their growing passion for evangelism and that you have a next-step opportunity for them at a place called Frontline (but don't scare them away with too much talk about the "E-word" or the spiritual gift of evangelism). Write down the date or give them a flyer with details for the next meeting. Assure them they'll enjoy it because they'll be with others who share their passion for reaching friends for

Christ. Be sure to get their name, address, phone number, and email address, and add them to your evangelism database so you can send them information about future events and opportunities. Developing ways to communicate directly with these people is very important, because they are the key to the rest of the 6-Stage Process. You can't become a truly contagious church without these contagious specialists.

## Seize Opportunities around Services

Once after our church completed a teaching series on evangelism we did something to make the most of the motivation and excitement people were feeling. We asked those who wanted to learn how they could get involved and take additional steps in reaching people to come meet with us for a few minutes immediately after the service.

What happened was incredible. About one out of ten people at the service went to the room—the elusive 10 percent! Very briefly, we challenged them to do three things:

1. If they hadn't already been through "basic training," we asked them to go to the next offering of the *Becoming a Contagious Christian* course, which was starting in a few weeks—or they could go through it with their small group. (This promoted Stage 4, training every believer.)
2. We challenged them not to miss our next Frontline meeting, which was coming up in four weeks (Stage 5, mobilizing the evangelism specialists throughout the church).
3. We encouraged them to consider serving as a leader of a seeker small group, which would begin by their attending the seeker leader's training, which was starting in two weeks (an example of Stage 6, outreach ministries and events, which we'll explore in the next chapter).

This focused teaching series and meeting produced the desired result—namely, finding many new Frontline members and evangelism leaders.

## Partner with the Church's Ministries

Another vital aspect of building this ministry is gaining the confidence and support of the directors of the various ministries throughout the church. They must see Frontline as their ally not their competitor.

For clarity, let's say your evangelism leader's name is Steve. Ideally, Steve needs to help the ministry directors find and appoint their own evangelistic leader from within their own context. This ministry leader will then be the primary contact that Steve should work with, as well as the ministry directors themselves, to strategize ways their ministry can move toward fulfilling its part of the church's evangelistic mission.

These evangelism leaders from the various ministries should attend all of the Frontline meetings and constantly encourage the right people in their own circles to attend the meetings with them. Gradually, this will help them develop evangelistic teams within their own ministries, and all of those team members should, in turn, become active in Frontline.

These evangelism leaders should also see to it that their ministry's director is kept informed of all evangelistic activities. Further, they should ensure that appropriate verbal and written announcements are made within their ministry to help maximize all outreach-oriented opportunities. In effect, these leaders should mirror within their own ministries the kinds of activities that Steve is engaged in churchwide.

One more note on gaining the trust and cooperation of the various ministries. Steve must tell the ministry directors, and then prove by his actions, that he will not hurt their ministry by trying to take away their volunteers. On the contrary, he is trying to serve them by training, encouraging, and informing their people, making them more effective in their own particular ministry. He wants them at the Frontline meeting so they'll be stronger in their service to their own ministry and therefore to the whole church.

That's not to say, of course, that people will never shift from primary service in that ministry to serving with other evangelistic ministries within the church. There will always be some movement and migration—which is natural and healthy. But this should not be Steve's intent nor should it become the reputation of the Frontline ministry. Further, that migration pattern should go both ways, with give-and-take from both the evangelism ministry and the other ministries, all for the goal of furthering the church and God's kingdom.

In addition, the directors of these ministries should know that Steve and his team are actively looking for ways to give broader exposure and support to their ministries' outreach initiatives at Frontline meetings. For example, if the women's ministry is sponsoring an evangelistic breakfast or the sports ministry is hosting an outreach-oriented 5K run,

Steve shouldn't leave them to fend for themselves. These are broad-based ministries for which evangelism is just one of many values, so when they engage in these kinds of efforts, they need all the encouragement they can get. Their outreach events provide great opportunities for the Frontline team to come alongside and, in a supportive role, help make their efforts a success.

So, for instance, Steve and his team need to go out of their way to get the details about the women's breakfast. Then they should talk it up at the Frontline meeting, hand out the flyers, encourage women in the group to attend with their friends, highlight opportunities for volunteers to get involved, and pray with the team for the event. Then, at the next Frontline meeting, they should let the women's ministry director or evangelistic leader report back on the event, sharing stories of how God used it.

This kind of cooperation, repeated time and again, will gain the enthusiastic support of the ministries throughout the church. It will position Frontline as a ministry that not only does its own team-building and outreach events but also serves and maximizes the evangelistic efforts of the ministries throughout the church. It will soon become known that the members of this team want to be on the front lines of the ministry action wherever the battle is being fought.

### Give Compelling Announcements

In your worship services, the evangelism leader or another sharp leader who is passionate about evangelism and involved with Frontline should give a compelling, upbeat announcement to spur interest in this team. This person should explain what the ministry is and invite everyone interested in reaching his or her friends for Christ to attend. The announcer should use first-person language, saying, "*We're* doing such and such.... *I* hope *I'll* see you there."

The senior pastor should also make announcements for the evangelism ministry on a regular basis (and thus needs to be kept up-to-date on what the ministry is doing and attend a meeting personally on occasion). In addition, the pastor should make Frontline attendance a point of application when preaching a sermon related to outreach. Attack from every angle!

Don't forget to add a winsome printed announcement or insert to the bulletin. Avoid the typical yawn-inducing: "The evangelism team will be sponsoring a pancake breakfast next Saturday morning. If you are on this team or want to join it, go to the booth after the service."

Instead, try something like this:

## GET IN ON THE ACTION!

If you have a passion for the adventure of reaching friends and family members for Christ, or if you'd like to catch some of that passion from others, join us next Saturday morning at the Frontline breakfast. We'll enjoy a great meal, hear some incredible stories of how God is using people in this church, and get the inside scoop on the upcoming Easter outreach. For more details or to sign up, stop by the Frontline booth after the service or call the church before Thursday. You won't want to miss this!

It's important to spread the net broadly. Tell listeners in no uncertain terms that your meetings are for anyone who wants to grow in the area of evangelism and that they don't have to have a spiritual gift of evangelism to come to the event.

Those who attend are a self-selecting group, undoubtedly a high concentration of whom have the evangelism gift—but let them discover this for themselves! If you talk about it too early, it may prevent many of them from attending. In fact, I know some members who have come to our group for years and love it, but who still insist they don't have the spiritual gift of evangelism. I just smile. Their ongoing passion and involvement reveal the truth. Besides, what's important is that they're trained, plugged in, growing, and taking risks for the sake of the gospel. Call it what you will—gift or no gift—God will use it!

### Send Invitations to the Entire Church

When you're first launching a new initiative like the *Becoming a Contagious Christian* training course or Frontline, a letter addressed to the entire congregation can go a long way toward creating excitement and involvement. Ideally the letter should be from both the pastor and the evangelism leader. Make it positive and optimistic, but serious in tone. People need to understand that this is not just another class or program; this is part of a new way of life that gets the church back to its age-old biblical mission.

This message will, of course, fit right in with the broader teaching and vision that people are beginning to notice in the church's worship services, membership meetings, small group training, Sunday school classes, and everywhere else they turn. It's all part of a God-glorifying evangelistic conspiracy!

## Connect with People in Spiritual Gifts Classes

I mentioned earlier the importance of every church training its members in the area of spiritual gifts. Courses like *Network* help them discover who God has made them to be and what he has made them to do. And about 10 percent of them will find out they have the spiritual gift of evangelism. Go after them!

How? The evangelism leader or someone else from the evangelism ministry should go to the class when the gift of evangelism is the subject. As part of the teaching or right before a break, tell participants that if they have this gift, they're blessed, because it's the most exciting one! (People with each spiritual gift think theirs is the best, so why can't we?) Then point them toward the evangelism training and the Frontline ministry. To maximize the opportunity, hand out invitations and then stay to talk with anyone who wants to know more.

Hopefully, the ministry that teaches these classes also keeps track of who attends and what their spiritual gifts are. If so, you can send follow-up mailings or have a key volunteer call the people who listed evangelism as one of their top gifts.

## Challenge Frontline Members to Expand the Team

One other easy-to-overlook place to build the Frontline ministry is at the team meetings themselves. If people are having a great experience, they'll want to bring others. Encourage them to do so, and provide invitations they can give to their friends to attend the next meeting. Tell them that they of all people—as evangelists—ought to be able to bring others. There is no more powerful way to expand this team than through the enthusiastic encouragement of its active members, because they're all highly contagious!

## A WORD ABOUT SCALE

It's important that we add that the Frontline ministry is in no way limited to any particular church size. Let's say, for example, you're in a congregation of eighty people. You cast the vision, live and instill the values, empower a leader, and begin to train the church. Lots of folks start getting more interested in reaching others, but one person in particular gets really fired up and wants to take it further. Believe it or not, you already have the makings of a Frontline ministry!

The two of you start to meet occasionally for breakfast, where you tell stories, share ideas, encourage each other, and pray together. One of the things you pray for is more team members.

The next month, you offer an evangelism training seminar. Word has gotten out about the training, and nine people from the congregation attend. At the end of the last session when you talk about Frontline (which, you assure the group, "still has room for a few more members"), two people show interest. Now there are four of you.

Then the first one leads a friend to Christ. Being the evangelism zealot that he is, he tells this new convert that a normal part of the Christian life, along with prayer and Bible study, is going to the Frontline meetings. Now you have five!

One loses interest, but two more join. Your team is really starting to get contagious! After a while, other people start hearing about this group, and they want to get in on the action. Tell them you *might* let them in if they can prove they're really serious about it. Some of them insist, so you allow them to join — and now there's a contagious movement afoot!

You might even want to consider pooling resources with other churches in town and do some combined Frontline events together. It's a great way to build momentum and to start seeing a broader impact on your entire region.

Whatever number your team starts with, that's okay. It doesn't take very many to "spur one another on toward love and good deeds" (Hebrews 10:24). But always keep your recruitment gears turning. As the participation and activity levels of this team of pacesetters goes up, so does the contagion factor of the entire church.

## A MEMORABLE WORD OF ENCOURAGEMENT

Our Frontline team had had a banner year. Members had shared many stories of how God used their efforts throughout the year. Many people had come to Christ through them.

Since it was early December and this would be the final meeting of the year, we decided to take a fresh approach to encouraging, thanking, and celebrating with the team. We arranged for eight of the people who had made commitments to Christ that year primarily through the efforts of Frontline members to join us for our breakfast meeting. These eight new Christians sat next to me on stools in front of the group, and I briefly interviewed each of them about the events that had led to their trusting in Christ. In particular, they described what a Frontline member had done to reach them with the good news about Jesus. Then, at the end of each story, we asked that team member to stand up and be recognized for allowing God to work through him or her. A man thanked his wife, a young boy expressed gratitude to his mother, and several others thanked their friends. In each case, the rest of the team responded with heartfelt affirmation and applause. They were celebrating with their teammates while at the same time making decisions that *they* would take similar steps during the next year to bring some of their own friends and family members to Christ.

As if that weren't enough encouragement, next came the highlight! We had asked Dr. Gilbert Bilezikian, the theologian who inspired the start of Willow Creek Community Church, to sit in on the meeting, and to say a few words in response to what he'd seen that morning.

With tear-filled eyes and voice trembling with emotion, Dr. Bilezikian stood in front of the group and said in his endearing French accent:

> I really didn't know what I was walking into today. I've been ambushed. You people have been shredding me. I was sitting there in pieces, because, ultimately, this is it. The programs, the schedules, the meetings. *This is what it's all about.*
>
> You people have reminded me of one of the most intensely impactful days in my life. When I was a child, we lived in Paris. That was my home, but my father had a summerhouse in the countryside in the western part of France.
>
> One day when I was twelve years old, in Paris, I saw the German troops coming. It was Hitler's army. They stayed in France for four years.
>
> They were the enemy. The oppressors. The occupants.
>
> But then on June 6, 1944, I turned the radio on and tuned to the BBC—which we were forbidden to do. And I learned that the Allied troops had debarked on the coastline not far from us in Normandy and that the invasion had started.
>
> It was one of the greatest days of my life—just to hear the news. And I knew that it was real, because for two or three weeks we had heard the roar of battle in the distance. The bombs, the cannons,

the constant noise, which became louder and louder as the battle approached.

Then one day we heard the tanks roll in, and I went down into the little village. And for the first time in my life I saw Americans. They were American soldiers who were there to push back the enemy.

*They were the front line of the invasion, and today you people reminded me of them. That's what you are doing—pushing back the gates of hell and making it count for eternity.*

Then he simply ended in prayer.

Everybody sat in stunned silence. God had visited us in a special way, inspiring and motivating all who were there. The interaction, the stories, and now the powerful words of this impassioned leader—this was Frontline at its best, and for those of us who were there, its impact will never be forgotten.

We all need moments of encouragement like this. I do, you do, and all of those in our churches with gifts or passion for evangelism need them. With God's help, let's do all we can to provide them in creative and effective ways.

## STAGE 5: KEY IDEA

*Inspire and mobilize contagious specialists throughout your church—the 10 percent.*

Since, then, we know what it is to fear the Lord, we try to persuade people.... For Christ's love compels us, because we are convinced that one died for all. (2 Corinthians 5:11, 14 TNIV)

## TO CONSIDER AND DISCUSS

1. Who are two or three church members you could invite to be part of a new Frontline ministry? What is it about them that makes you think they're the right kind of people?

2. How can you begin to gather these people informally and see if the group's evangelistic temperature begins to heat up?

3. Where are some of the broader arenas and opportunities you can use to start promoting and inviting others into this new ministry?

4. Who are some of the people inside or outside your church you could draw on as resources to help you teach and inspire this Frontline group?

5. Consider two or three topics you think would be helpful to discuss with the evangelism enthusiasts in your church.

CHAPTER SEVEN

# STAGE 6: UNLEASH AN ARRAY OF OUTREACH MINISTRIES AND EVENTS

"HI, MARK. DO YOU REMEMBER me?"

I wanted to say yes. I strained my memory in an effort to justify saying yes. I opened my mouth hoping to get out a "yes." But I just couldn't honestly tell her I remembered her.

"Umm, you're going to have to help me out a bit," I said to the young woman standing in front of me by our church's pond, her hair dripping wet.

"We met briefly about four years ago when you and your wife were looking for an apartment down in Streamwood," she informed me. "I worked for the real estate company that was showing the apartments. But you never came back...."

"I'm sorry, we ended up moving into another area," I said, still reaching back into the dusty fringes of my memory.

"That's okay," she said. "You did what you were sent to do!"

"I did?" I said, feeling a mix of relief and curiosity.

"You sure did. Don't you remember that you started telling me about this church? You told me it was a great place to meet new friends and to learn about the Bible."

"It's starting to come back to me...."

"You also gave me one of those little business card–sized invitations to the church. Remember, it had a map on it," she said.

"Of course—I try to carry them with me all the time," I replied, silently deepening my resolve to continue that habit.

"Well, God used that conversation, as well as a later one I had with someone else from the church, to get me to visit. After I was here for a while, I understood the message, asked Jesus to forgive my sins, and today I was baptized! When I saw you out here during the baptism service, I decided to come over and update you on what happened. Thanks for letting God use you!"

"You're more than welcome," I said enthusiastically, as I gave her a hug and congratulated her further. "That's really amazing!"

## THE POWER OF A COMBINED EFFORT

This young woman's experience was a great example of the synergy that can develop between individual evangelistic efforts—in this case, my own very limited efforts—and larger outreach events. I have seen many of these examples over the years, some out of my experience, and many more in the lives of friends.

I'm friends with a couple named Tom and Lynn, for instance, who along with Tom's two sisters tried again and again to help Tom's parents understand the gospel. They kept up their evangelism efforts for years, including numerous conversations and multiple invitations to our church's outreach services. But it wasn't until one service in particular, when evangelist Luis Palau was speaking, that Tom's parents finally were ready. On that very night they both—a couple in their mid sixties—made Christ their forgiver and leader. Again, it was personal evangelism combined with broader team efforts that led them to cross the line of faith. About a year later I had the thrill of celebrating with them by the pond as they, too, were baptized.

I recently called my own father, Orland Mittelberg, and asked for details about how he became a Christian. True to form, it was the pairing of the personal witness of his chief petty officer in the navy, a man named Bill Abraham, mixed with a larger "outreach event" in Memphis, Tennessee, in the mid-1940s. That event was a revival meeting hosted by Youth for Christ, at which the famous evangelist Charles E. Fuller spoke. My dad attended the meeting at the urging of Bill, as well as his own mother, Effa, who was praying daily for his salvation. He told me he sat way up in the balcony "in order to stay at a safe distance." But when the invitation was given at the end of the night, he raised his hand, and Charles Fuller pointed up at him and said, "I see your hand up there in the balcony, sailor boy. God bless you!" Before my father fully knew what was happening, he was standing down in front, praying with a counselor to receive Christ. His life—as well as the life of his family—has never been the same since!

Are you beginning to see why I often describe this combination of individual evangelism efforts and larger outreach events as a synergistic one-two punch? The impact can be incredible! The power of this pairing of personal and team efforts has been proven time and again, as far back as the Samaritan woman at the well in John 4, who first told her friends all Jesus had said (personal evangelism), and then brought them to the well to hear Jesus themselves (team evangelism)—and all the way through to today at Graham and Palau crusades, and at the evangelistic church services hosted by many churches.

## THE DOWNSIDE OF MAKING MEMBERS WORK ALONE

Now let me state the flip side. As I illustrated out of my own experience in chapter one, it's hard to do evangelism alone, without the supporting efforts of a broader church or ministry. In fact, it's getting increasingly difficult as our culture becomes more and more secular and people move increasingly further away from the truth and teachings of Jesus. Between us and the people we want to reach are walls of confusion, misinformation, competing ideologies, and the lures of sin—all of which conspire to keep them far from God and continually moving in the wrong direction.

It's against that backdrop that many churches send out their people to fight the battle completely on their own. "You can do it," they say in effect. "If God is for you ... *then why do you need our help?*" So they send out their unprepared sheep among the hungry wolves and hope for the best.

As a result, many sincere Christians, with fear and trembling, wander around the landscape without the encouragement or leadership of an evangelistic church—Stages 1 through 3. They also lack the training we talked about in Stage 4, the camaraderie and support we discussed in Stage 5, and certainly the synergistic group efforts we'll explore next under Stage 6, as we "UNLEASH an Array of Outreach Ministries and Events."

The outcome? Tragically, though not surprisingly, in far too many cases the wolves are having the sheep for lunch. We need to start preparing our people better, reinforcing their efforts with a team, and strategically partnering with them by developing supplemental outreach ministries and events.

We must work together to accomplish what none of us can or should do alone.

## THE IMPACT OF TEAM EVANGELISM

The larger, united outreach events of Stage 6 can actually become engines that drive the values and skills we've been trying to build into our people in the earlier stages. It was, for example, the fact that the church had a weekly outreach service that made it easy for my wife and me to talk to the woman at the apartment complex. The repeated event became the occasion for a natural invitation — and topic of conversation.

George Barna observed years ago that, according to his studies, one out of four adults in the United States would go to church if a friend would invite them.[1] (Since then some have suggested that the number is even higher.) This is exciting on two counts. First, if your church would put forth the effort to produce some high-quality, biblically relevant evangelistic services or events, a lot of your friends would be willing to attend. But, second, for every four invitations, three people would say no — which means your event has generated three conversations about spiritual matters that probably wouldn't have taken place otherwise!

We tell participants in the *Becoming a Contagious Christian* course that if they invite their friend to an event and they're turned down, that's okay — just turn it into an opportunity to talk. Say something like, "I'm sorry you won't be able to attend our Christmas Eve service with us. I'm curious, though, how does your family observe the holiday? What does that day mean to you?"

Whatever the event is — from a Christmas service to a contemporary Christian music concert — it can be the catalyst for hundreds of conversations throughout your community, as well as being used by God to bear fruit in and of itself.

But the natural question is: How can we put together these special events? And with whom? Who would have the time, energy, and creativity to develop and promote such programs? The answer lies in the link between Stages 5 and 6. Let me illustrate.

## A MINISTRY CASE IN POINT

Several years back, some of us at our church began to think about starting evangelistic small groups. At the time we had a strong small group ministry at our church, but the groups were designed for discipling believers, not for outreach. We were intrigued by the idea that we could start groups primarily for spiritual seekers.

Right around that time we interviewed a young pastor from Indianapolis named Garry Poole, who said he wanted to shift his focus more toward evangelism, which he said was his primary gift and passion. So we talked about this idea of building what we called seeker small groups. Garry was instantly excited about the idea and told us of similar groups he'd started while in college. Before long, Garry was on our team with the primary charge of starting these new, outreach-focused small groups. But immediately upon joining us, Garry faced the question I raised earlier: Where should he start, and with whom?

### "The Usual Suspects"

In most church situations you'd have to start pretty much from scratch in order to build a seeker small group ministry. You might have a few people already teaching small groups who could "move over" and try to lead evangelistic groups. But this typically doesn't work very well, because it was their shepherding gifts that got them into that role in the first place—and people with shepherding gifts don't usually have evangelism gifts as well.

You could also try recruiting from an existing evangelistic visitation team. However, the people on these teams often lack the patience and the interpersonal approach needed to sustain long-term friendships, meet weekly, and gently move people along in their journey to faith. If that were their approach, they probably wouldn't fit a traditional visitation team very well.

Where else could you look? In most church settings there aren't a lot of other options. You could make general announcements, but you'd very likely get a low response. And those who might respond would, in many cases, lack the necessary skills and training. So your chances of succeeding would be very limited.

## The New Scenario

But what if you were in a church that had been instilling the value of evangelism into its members for a long time? A place where hearts were getting bigger for lost people? A setting where every attendee was being trained for relational evangelism, and where those with gifts or a passion for outreach were being pulled together and encouraged on a regular basis? And what if those names and phone numbers were readily accessible in a churchwide database? That would be a different picture entirely!

This is the scenario into which Garry entered. The stage had already been set. His ministry was already poised to win.

## A Team in Waiting

Stepping back for a moment, remember that evangelism folks are *action people.* You dare not get them trained and joined together on a team, and then fail to give them something to do. These men and women will be chomping at the bit, and if you don't give them a meaningful place to expend all of that spiritual energy, they may become downright dangerous! One way or another, they'll create some action.

This is a pretty good picture of what was evolving in our situation. We had this wonderful thing called Frontline, but limited opportunities in terms of specific ministry roles. This is one of the challenging aspects of emphasizing personal evangelism—it's so *personal!* It's not easy to build *group* efforts around it.

Our troops were trained and looking for some fresh battlefronts. No kidding, one member used to call me and say, "Give me something to do, Mark. I want some action. I'm ready to get bloodied for God!"

Whoa! It was certainly time to offer up some well-thought-through opportunities.

Can you see what was shaping up? Supply and demand were both growing rapidly. The *supply* was a team ready to do something; the *demand* was, among other things, an outreach-oriented small group ministry that desperately needed leaders. We just had to get the two sides together—which was a primary purpose of the Frontline ministry in the first place.

## The Natural Next Step

So at our next Frontline meeting, I introduced our newest staff member, Garry Poole, and together Garry and I cast the vision for this new seeker small group ministry.

I explained how we wanted to serve visitors to our services who were not yet in a relationship with anyone in the church. I described how these new groups would provide a place for these people to get to know several other people who had similar questions, as well as a couple of knowledgeable Christians (namely *them*) with whom they could develop trust, ask questions, and move forward spiritually to the point of trusting Christ. Then, after enfolding many of these church visitors, we planned to broaden the circle and reach into our neighborhoods and workplaces to attract people into these groups who hadn't yet come to the church.

Garry then communicated the incredible potential in this approach by telling stories of how he had built seeker groups in college dorms and, over time, saw several of his friends—including some highly unlikely candidates—join God's family. He gave specifics on how we planned to train many of those in Frontline and help them attract seekers into the groups they would be starting.

By the end of that meeting the team was inspired and ready for a call to action. We didn't have to persuade them that evangelism is important or that God could use them to be difference makers. That groundwork had long been laid. These people were ready to build on that foundation and make things happen.

So Garry invited all of those interested in being part of this new ministry to sign up for the upcoming seeker small group training. About a third of them registered to take the next step. In the days that followed, Garry interviewed these people, selected the ones he felt were right for the role, and began training them. Within a matter of a few weeks, he had thirty newly trained leaders.

Again, it's the *process* that's of importance here, not the particular numbers. We may have drawn thirty qualified candidates out of a large pool of Frontline folks; in your situation it might be four out of a pool of sixteen. But four qualified leaders who already own the values and who have been through the basic evangelism training is a pretty good start!

This is how our seeker small group ministry was jump-started—and it hasn't slowed down since. Over the years since its beginning, hundreds have come to faith through the efforts of its faithful leaders. In fact, the great majority of people who stay in their groups end up trusting Christ, usually within about a year. Many other churches are now starting the same kind of ministries as well, based on guidance from the book Garry later wrote, called *Seeker Small Groups*.[2] He also developed his basic approach into a unique small group curriculum called *Tough Questions*, designed for groups of seekers as well as for Christians who are wrestling with their beliefs.[3]

Outreach ministries flow naturally out of a robust, broad-based evangelism ministry like the one I prescribed in Stage 5. In your church this might include things like a visitation team, a visitor callback ministry, a new kind of seeker Sunday school class, Alpha groups, or a seeker small group ministry like the one I've been discussing here. The possibilities are virtually endless.

In addition to supporting these larger ministries, the Frontline ministry should also sponsor a variety of high-quality outreach events to which your people can bring their friends. Some of these will be church-wide, like a major evangelistic concert, movie, or drama presentation. Others will be ministry specific, like the women's ministry's outreach breakfast or the sports ministry's 5K run I mentioned earlier. Still more will be niche specific, such as events targeted to narrower age or special interest groups, like an event for junior high students or a seminar designed to reach Jewish people.

This broad array of outreach ministries and events makes up the thrust of Stage 6.

## THE FRONTLINE MINISTRY STRUCTURE: A MINISTRY OF MULTIPLE TEAMS

Frontline is the overarching ministry that can help inspire, shape, empower, and execute these outreach activities throughout the church. This will include those activities and teams directly under the evangelism ministry's own control, as well as those it helps in cooperation with the other ministries of the church. Earlier I described this as being cross-departmental. Figure 7.1 shows what the structure looks like.

Frontline functions best as an umbrella ministry with two kinds of teams and activities under it. The first, shown on the left side, is the evangelism department's own specialized ministries and events. This would include things like a seeker small group ministry, any outreach-oriented visitation teams, and many others. The second category, on the right side, includes all of the church's other ministries and events related to evangelism.

So when the women's ministry is sponsoring an outreach breakfast, it becomes a vital interest to the Frontline ministry. The evangelism leader

Figure 7.1

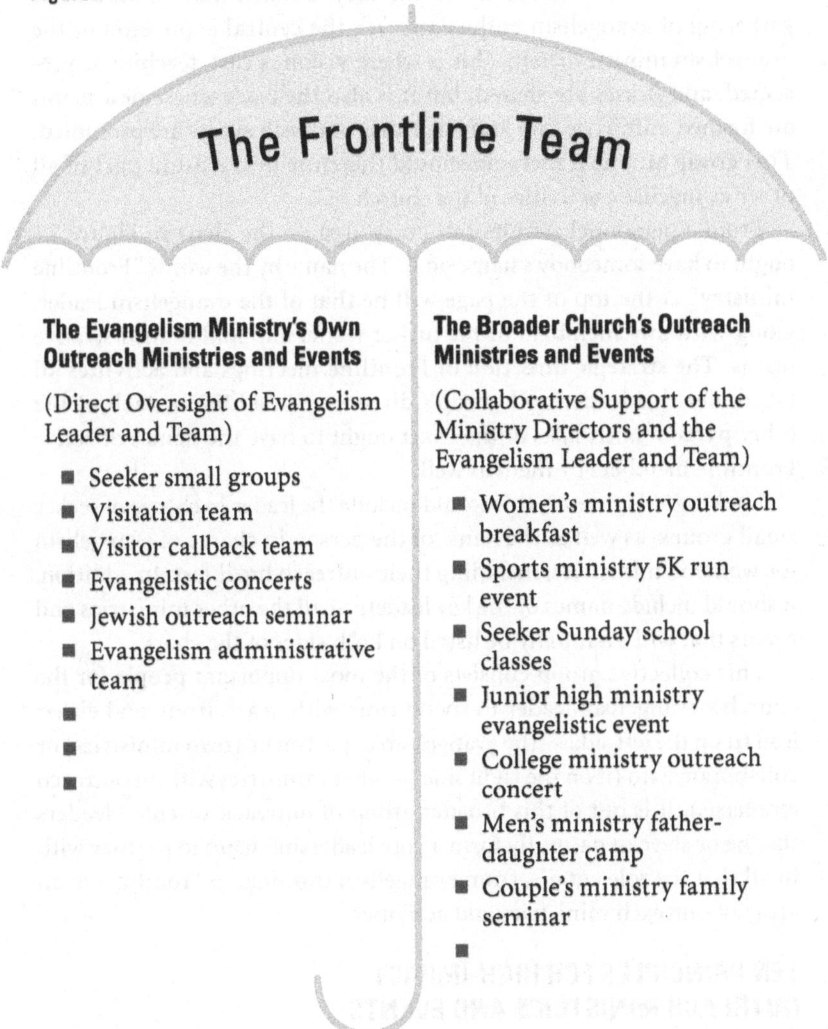

## The Frontline Team

**The Evangelism Ministry's Own Outreach Ministries and Events**

(Direct Oversight of Evangelism Leader and Team)

- Seeker small groups
- Visitation team
- Visitor callback team
- Evangelistic concerts
- Jewish outreach seminar
- Evangelism administrative team
- 
- 
- 

**The Broader Church's Outreach Ministries and Events**

(Collaborative Support of the Ministry Directors and the Evangelism Leader and Team)

- Women's ministry outreach breakfast
- Sports ministry 5K run event
- Seeker Sunday school classes
- Junior high ministry evangelistic event
- College ministry outreach concert
- Men's ministry father-daughter camp
- Couple's ministry family seminar
- 

and his or her team is not in charge of it; but they can supply ideas, support, and possibly even personnel to help pull it off well. The women's ministry still owns and runs the event, but their efforts are turbocharged by the larger team of people who have outreach expertise and passion.

As you can see, the Frontline ministry is much more than a mere gathering of evangelism enthusiasts. It's the central expression of the evangelism ministry itself. This is where vision is cast, teaching is presented, and stories are shared; but it is also the place where new teams are formed, ministries are launched, and outreach events are promoted. This group and its leadership should therefore be a natural part of all other evangelistic activities of the church.

From a personnel standpoint, every area on the chart in Figure 7.1 ought to have somebody's name on it. The name by the words "Frontline ministry" at the top of the page will be that of the evangelism leader, along with any members of his or her leadership and administrative teams. The strategic direction of Frontline meetings and activities all fall under this leader and group's direction. In addition, each of the other parts of both sides of the chart ought to have the names of active Frontline members by them as well.

Looking at Figure 7.1, this would include the leader in charge of seeker small groups, as well as the name of the person in charge of evangelism for women's ministries, including their outreach breakfast. In addition, it should include names of the key leaders of all the other ministries and events that will eventually be listed on both sides of the chart.

This collective group consists of the most important people for the church's evangelism leader to spend time with, learn from, and either lead (if on the left side — the evangelism department's own ministries) or collaborate with (if on the right side — other ministries with an outreach emphasis). It is out of this broader group of outreach-oriented leaders that he or she can naturally form a core leadership team to partner with in all that the role entails, from evangelism training, to Frontline, to an array of outreach ministries and activities.

## TEN PRINCIPLES FOR HIGH-IMPACT OUTREACH MINISTRIES AND EVENTS

Let's look at ten principles for planning and leading outreach ministries and events for maximum impact:

### 1. Define Your Purpose and Goals

The first question to ask is, "What are we trying to do?" Too often we assume that we know when in reality we don't. The purpose must be clear to both the leaders and the team.

Bill Hybels tells of three men who decided to put their resources together to start a new restaurant. The vision seemed clear until they got to the point of interior design:

"We'll need lots of oriental fans and dragons on the walls," said the first man. "We can't have a Chinese restaurant without them!"

"What are you talking about?" shot back the second man. "This isn't going to be a Chinese restaurant! It's going to be Italian — the only good kind of eating establishment!"

"Reckon you're both wrong," said the third man. "What we're building is a Texas barbecue, with lots of cowboy boots and saddles and pictures of horses all over the walls — and country-and-western music playing too!"

See the problem? We often wait too long to state what we each want to accomplish. When it comes to outreach, the principle is the same: We need to talk about what we want to do until we reach clarity and consensus. Is this an early, primer event that we hope will get people started on a spiritual quest? Or is it a middle-range event, designed to help seekers progress in their spiritual journeys? Or is it a net-drawing event, designed to help people make the decision to cross the line of faith and commit their lives to Christ?

These three purposes, though each legitimate, are about as different from each other as are Chinese, Italian, and Texas-barbecue restaurants!

It's also important, once the broad purpose is determined, to go a step further and articulate what your specific goals are for an event. What would success look like? Do you hope to expose a certain number of new people to the church? Are you aiming to help a particular number of seekers take a next step in their spiritual journeys? Would you like to launch a predetermined number of evangelistic Bible studies or seeker small groups? Is your aim to see a certain number of individuals put their trust in Christ before they go home? It is hard to hit a target you can't see, and difficult to evaluate your efforts and improve the next time around if you have no agreed-upon mark you're shooting for.

## 2. Know Who You're Trying to Reach

It's important to decide whom your outreach efforts are aimed to serve: children, singles, marrieds, empty nesters, retirees? A certain segment of the community, residents in an apartment complex, students at a particular university, an international or ethnic group, punk rockers, the coffee klatch at the local café? Once you know who you want to reach you'll be able to begin shaping your approach. As Rick Warren said, "The Bible determines our message, but our target determines when, where, and how we communicate it."[4]

Also, once you know what group of people you want to impact, it's vital that you *get to know a few of them*! Find out what makes them tick. What are their questions? What interests them? What issues do they wrestle with? Get to know their heritage. Learn their language—find out what words and concepts connect with them and which ones make their eyes glaze over. Then speak with them, presenting God's truth, but in their own language. Design ministries and events that will relate to them.

For example, when I brought in Stan Telchin, the author of the powerful book, *Betrayed!*[5] to speak for an outreach to Jewish people, he helped me understand that a word I use frequently will alienate many Jewish people. The term? *Christ*. Stan explained to me that this is a problem word because cruel people sometimes call Jewish people "Christ-haters," or even worse, "Christ-killers." So, he explained, you can spend your whole life trying to correct their misconceptions of who Christ really is, or you can sidestep the problem by referring to him as "Jesus." Stan recommended the latter!

What a valuable lesson—one I try to apply whenever I talk to Jewish people. And it's a good example of the kind of learning we need to gain in order to lovingly relate to the people we hope to reach.

Know your target. Become "all things to all people" (1 Corinthians 9:22 TNIV) so that the ministries and events you design will hit the mark.

### 3. Communicate Your Purpose and Your Intended Audience

Once you've determined your purpose and whom you hope to reach, it's crucial to communicate this information to the rest of the team and throughout the church body, and especially to guest speakers who will be involved in the event.

We once almost had a disaster due to a lack of clarity in communication related to sports outreach. Several days before the event, Lee Strobel and I decided to go to the radio studio and meet with the sports broadcaster we had invited to speak. We just wanted to touch base and make certain everything was on track for the Saturday event. But in the course of talking together, this man casually mentioned that he was planning to make a strong appeal at the end of his talk and invite people to come forward and receive Christ.

Were we ever glad we were having that conversation! We assured him that our goal, like his, was to help people reach the point where they would respond to the gospel and embrace Christ. But we also explained that we didn't see this single sports-related event as the place to try to make all of that happen. Rather, we saw it as one link in the chain — an early one — that would lead naturally to further steps, including attendance at the church's services.

He understood and supported our goals and, like us, was glad we'd talked before the event. And, to finish the story, his message at the breakfast was a home run, and we heard stories afterward about how the event helped some attenders take steps forward in their spiritual journeys.

You can never go too far in making certain your entire team understands and supports your goals and purposes for every outreach event and ministry.

## 4. Innovate Fresh Approaches

Many years ago some friends and I tried to rent the main auditorium at our local university for an outreach concert. But the room, we discovered, was under construction and unavailable. We were tempted to give up the idea, but instead rented the front steps and lawn of the building and had an outdoor concert. The impact of that event turned out to be greater than it would have been if we'd been able to use the auditorium inside.

When I helped bring a Christian expert on the cults and sects, Kurt Van Gordon, to our town to speak about the unbiblical teachings of The Way International, I was disappointed that none of the people I was befriending in that group were willing to come hear him. So after his seminar was over, I drove Kurt to the house where the group's leaders lived. They didn't look very excited to see us, but they let us in, and we ended up talking with them and challenging their aberrant teachings for over an hour. This was just one of the ways my friends and I resisted their influence in our community, and within months their whole team packed up and left town.

When Lee Strobel and I first decided to host a debate between a Christian and an atheist, our idea was nearly shut down. I had been told by some well-meaning believers that an event of this kind should never be done inside a church because of the damage it could do to the church's reputation. I thought and prayed about it for a long time, and I finally decided to set aside convention and do the event in our main auditorium. By God's grace, it turned out to be one of the most powerful events in the history of our church.

One time we invited Phillip Johnson, renowned law professor at the University of California at Berkeley, to come and do a seminar related to his book, *Darwin on Trial*.[6] We knew it would be a challenge to get the right people to come hear about this topic at a church, but we decided to target the teachers in the community anyway. So, in partnership with the book's publisher, we gave each of our church's high school ministry's student leaders a copy of *Darwin on Trial* to give to their teachers, along with a personalized invitation to the event. Then we mailed a letter to every science teacher in each of the communities surrounding our church, inviting them to come to the seminar and to enjoy reserved VIP seating. We also assured them that they could raise the first questions during a question-and-answer time at the end. Finally, we told the media all that we had done, and warned them that this could turn into a very controversial gathering! Well, that got them excited, and they ran some articles talking about and debating the merits of this upcoming seminar.

The result? An event that might have attracted a small number of people ended up drawing a crowd of 4,300—and the evidence for an Intelligent Designer was communicated to multitudes of people, many of whom wouldn't normally darken the doors of a church.

These are just a few examples from my own experience that prove you don't have to stay within the confines of convention when planning outreach events. Instead, get your creative types together and ask, "How could we do this thing in a fresh and exciting way? What could we try that nobody else is trying? What kind of innovation might capture the attention of the community and turn out to be a coup for the kingdom?"

An event may be risky, but if it's within biblical parameters and seems to be a wise and God-honoring approach, why not try it? Who would have thought of having a bunch of Christ-followers stand up in the middle of Jerusalem, the city in which Jesus had been crucified just a few weeks earlier, and have them talk about him to the crowds who were gathering there? What kind of a strategy was that? Unconventional? Controversial? On the edge? Yes, all of that—and according to Acts 2, it was led and powerfully used by God!

## 5. Design the Event to Fulfill the Purpose and Hit the Target

The room was warm. The large-print hymnals were easy to reach. We sang familiar, encouraging songs with words like "Happy day, happy day, when Jesus washed my sins away! He taught me how to watch and pray and live rejoicing ev'ry day."[7] The sanctuary was clean, the lighting bright, the sound clear and fairly loud, making it easy to hear everything that was said. The minister wore a robe and spoke slowly and deliberately. The message was right out of the Bible, straightforward yet simple. Before the service ended, we recited the Apostles' Creed and the Lord's Prayer. Then we sang "What a Friend We Have in Jesus" and heard the benediction—and the service was over.

*It was one of the most relevant church services I've ever attended.*

Why? Because it was the chapel service at the nursing home of my grandmother Effa Mittelberg, and most of the people attending were in their nineties and had grown up in traditional churches. Whether or not they all knew Christ, they knew this was what church was supposed to be like. The message was clear, and the method of presenting it was right on target. To have tried anything remotely contemporary would have been irrelevant and even offensive.

Two weeks later I walked into a crowded gymnasium. I was handed a bag of popcorn on the way in, along with a program that said, "Axis at the Movies." The room was dark, noisy, energetic, and filled with edgy music pouring through a high-powered sound system. Soon the stage lights came on and the music kicked in at an even higher level for the portion of the service labeled "Band Jam." In the fast-moving sequence that followed, young leaders stood and greeted us, led us in a few upbeat worship songs, performed a true-to-life drama, and showed clips from a recent movie. Then a casually dressed teacher got up and presented an honest, hard-hitting message about how we can all search for truth— and find it—in the Bible and ultimately in Christ.

*This, too, was one of the most relevant church services I've ever experienced.*

Why? Because this was a ministry designed to reach people in their twenties who grew up with these kinds of media and communication styles, and who needed to hear biblical teaching in language they could understand.

Relevancy is a relative concept. Different audiences, different events— both designed for the people they were intended to reach. The message was the same, but the methods vastly different. This is the missionary principle of contextualization, which says we need to communicate the uncompromised gospel, but put it in language and illustrations that will make it clear to the people we're talking to. Or, as Paul puts it in 1 Corinthians 9:22–23 (TNIV), we must "become all things to all people ... for the sake of the gospel."

It'll take hard work and a lot of adjustments along the way, but make certain the events you plan and promote fit the people and the purpose for which you're creating them.

## 6. Do Only What You Can Do Well

I've had a number of conversations with church leaders who've said, "We're getting serious about reaching people for Christ, so we're going to start offering high-impact outreach services every Saturday night, starting next month."

Something inside me cringes. "Umm, I'm curious: Have you ever put together a service like you're planning — one your team felt great about afterward? And if so, have you ever tried doing two or three in a row, with only six days in between them to get ready for the next one?"

Often these leaders had never even tried one, or if they had, they weren't very happy with it. And now they're signing up to do fifty-two of them each year! My advice is to slow down. Plan a single outreach event. Or, at most, start with a series of two or three. Brainstorm them thoroughly. Prepare to the hilt. Invest prayer, resources, personnel, creativity, and energy to make sure you're ready. Muster all the excellence you can to make it as good as it can be. This will help you fulfill Colossians 4:5, which says, "Be wise in the way you act toward outsiders; make the most of every opportunity."

While we need to avoid becoming paralyzed by perfectionism, we live in a culture where, in spite of all its moral blunders, technical excellence is assumed. In every arena of life, whether business, leisure, or entertainment, people are used to things being done well. So if you want to do outreach that will command attention and respect, start with fewer events and make them great. Make them so good that those who attend without bringing their friends will regret it for weeks! Then gradually expand the number and variety of events, while simultaneously growing and deepening the team that makes them happen.

## 7. Integrate Your Efforts with Other Events and Opportunities

Don't think of your outreach events in isolation. View them as important threads in the overall fabric of your church. Discuss some key questions with your planning team: How does this effort fit into the church's overarching mission and goals? How could you adjust the timing of this event to help it create more synergy with the other ministries and the church overall? What will precede it that you could build on? What will follow this event that it could feed into?

For example, the *Darwin on Trial* event I discussed earlier was part of a larger plan. We'd scheduled a series of Sunday sermons called "Christianity: Fact or Fiction?" and we knew that the last week would focus on the evidence for a divine Creator. So to build upon and expand the impact of that series, we scheduled the event for the Sunday night of that final week.

We were pretty confident that the momentum of the series, combined with the questions people have about human origins, would make this a high-interest event. But we wanted to move people to take further steps in the right direction. These included: (1) the opportunity to ask questions of Phillip Johnson during the program; (2) a place to write down questions and then receive a follow-up call from a member of our team; (3) strong urging from the platform to join a small group designed to discuss their questions and concerns—with sign-ups available that night; and (4) encouragement to attend the new message series beginning the following Sunday.

This last one was important, because we knew there would be lots of folks there who had not yet attended a service. So we worked to help them understand that this is a church where people with doubts and questions are welcomed, and that the new weekend topic was an important one for them. Our goal was to not only serve them that night, but also to draw them back so we could serve them in additional ways—all the way to the point of salvation!

Another example of integrating your efforts is developing an overall outreach plan around your Christmas and Easter services. These are peak visitor attendance times, yet many churches fail to think strategically about what happens immediately afterward. Carloads of visiting friends and family members sit through the holiday service, which they probably enjoy and learn from. But then they may hear an uninspiring announcement for the following Sunday: "Next week we're going to continue our twelve-part series on the Minor Prophets," the announcer says, "as Pastor Bob teaches us more about the repeated rebellion of God's people and the awful punishment that followed. We hope you'll join us at 9:00 or 11:00 a.m." The average visitor appreciates the warning. A weekend at the lake — or even just at home cleaning the garage — is sounding better than ever!

How much more effective could it be to start a new series the following week that would be interesting to your visiting friends? It may actually *be* a study on the Minor Prophets, presented in a way that shows their relevance to daily life. It might include a title like, "Learning from the Mistakes of Others," or "Developing a Real-World Faith." Announce it in a winsome way and put an attractive invitation into visitors' hands that gives them the topic, the service times, and the location with directions (since they may have gotten a ride with their friends or relatives and don't know how to get back to the church).

Granted, they won't all come back. Many will wait for the next holiday or special event before returning. But what if five out of fifty visitors come back? And what if you do the same thing at the next holiday services and some of these forty-five people, along with a few new guests, start seeing that your church is a place to learn about things that really matter? That next time around you might retain eight more. Now you're gaining some momentum!

The earlier you can introduce this integrated thinking into your event planning, the better you'll be able to shape what you do for maximum synergy and impact.

## 8. Promote Your Events with Precision and Power

First, promote your events with *precision*. Watch out that you don't fall into what is known in business circles as a "bait and switch." The term comes from an unethical sales practice where, for example, a low-end home appliance is promoted at a rock-bottom price, even though that appliance is not really available. The goal is to lure customers in and then "sell them up" to more expensive — and more profitable — appliances.

The same thing happens all too often in Christian circles. We say, "Come to a sports breakfast," when in reality it will be a thinly disguised evangelistic rally. Perceptive seekers feel tricked and leave angry. Many will never come back.

Promotion must be done with integrity. If an event is advertised as a sports breakfast, then spend the vast majority of the time talking about sports. Weave in a little spiritual content, but measure it carefully. If you want to make it more evangelistically intense, then communicate it in a way that doesn't hide your intentions. I'm not saying you need to put on the posters, "An event designed to convert you to Christ!" but a gentle hint will do, like, "Get the inside scoop on the exciting career of [well-known Christian athlete], and hear the behind-the-scenes details of his fascinating spiritual journey." It's far better to have fewer people attend who have a sense of what they're coming to, than to have lots of people show up but walk away feeling duped.

One more thought on accuracy in communication: Beware of promoting events as something new when they're really the same old thing with only a few cosmetic changes. I remember Lee Strobel calling me at home one Sunday afternoon in exasperation. "I just came from a church that advertised itself as being relevant and geared to people who don't go to church," he said. "But boy, did they ever miss the target!" This was a rare tone for Lee, who is normally buoyant and upbeat, but he was outraged. Why? Because he had come to Christ largely through church services that really were relevant and designed for outsiders. He couldn't help imagining how this place might have derailed his own spiritual journey. He was simply putting himself in the shoes of any seeker who fell for this church's advertisements and attended its services.

Lee described this experience in his book *Inside the Mind of Unchurched Harry and Mary*:

> The service started with someone asking the congregation to sing along with a chorus for which no lyrics were provided. Regular attenders, of course, knew the words, but I felt awkward. Other hymns, accompanied by an organ, dated from 1869, 1871, and 1874, with such lyrics as, "Heav'nly portals loud with hosannas ring." The microphones were tinny and the sound cut in and out, prompting a vocalist at one point to pause with an embarrassed smile in the middle of a song.
>
> During the announcement time, a pastor directed newcomers to fill out a card "so we can put you on our mailing list." He also jokingly but with an air of desperation offered a $100 bounty if members of the church's board would attend a meeting that afternoon so they would finally have a quorum. He added with frustration, "We need to approve the painting of the church, which should have been done last year, and the painting of the house I live in, which should have been painted last year, too."

> The sermon, part of a series called "Issues in Christian Discipleship" ... talked about denying oneself to follow Christ, but there wasn't much explanation of what that meant on a practical, day-to-day level. He did say the Christian life has its benefits, although he didn't elaborate on what they were. At the conclusion, he offered only two steps for people to take: Either turn over your life to Christ, or commit yourself to deeper discipleship.[8]

Maybe we can get away with these kinds of things among believers. *Maybe.* But these tactics will never fly with most unchurched visitors who are considering Christianity. We'll leave them confounded and confused—and then they'll leave us.

Don't promise relevancy until you're ready to deliver it. Be precise and honest in what you promote. Otherwise, it may be your only chance.

Also, concerning promoting with *power*, no matter how powerful your event is going to be, it can't have a maximum impact if it's not filled with the right people. You have to put as much energy into getting the word out as you do in putting the event together.

There are many ways to do this. Mailings, websites, email blasts, radio and TV spots, billboards, signs, flyers, and letters to people moving into the area can all have an impact. But here's one that's often overlooked: high quality and well-worded printed pieces for your members to use as tools to invite their friends. This kind of "advertising" often has more impact than the impersonal kind, because it comes with the endorsement and encouragement of a trusted friend, not to mention the offer of a ride along with a nice brunch or tasty pizza before or after the event! (And keep in mind that Outreach, Inc. can save you a lot of time and effort with the various communication tools they offer—see: www.outreach.com.)

In addition, I'd recommend printing some high-quality business card–sized invitations that list the church's name, address, phone number, and website, as well as service times and a map on the back to help people get there. Keep these cards on display at an info booth outside your sanctuary, and encourage all attendees—including visitors—to use them to invite their friends. It was one of these cards that I had given to the woman I mentioned at the beginning of the chapter.

Gather your team around a table to brainstorm creative, effective, and honest ways to get the word out to as many people as possible. This will multiply the impact of all of your outreach efforts.

## 9. Measure and Evaluate Results — and Improve Next Time

Don't consider your outreach event complete until you have talked about it with your team to see what can be learned from the experience and what can be done better next time. This takes humility, gentleness, and a high level of trust among team members. They need to know that the purpose of evaluation is not to judge or make anybody feel bad. In fact, much of what will happen will be celebration over the good things that occurred, along with a lot of laughter over funny things that happened along the way. But in looking back, priceless lessons can be drawn out and applied in order to help make the next event even more effective. If you don't evaluate, you will keep making the same mistakes over and over, and you will severely limit your ability to maximize your team efforts in the future.

More than just evaluating the programming or teaching elements, we need to measure actual results in terms of the number of people affected, and then compare these results to our original purposes for the event. Was this an introductory event designed with the hope of exposing a hundred new people to the church? If that was the goal, then make sure you count how many showed up and compare the numbers. If eighty-four actually came, how does the team feel about this? Was the expectation of a hundred too high — or was there a problem with the planning or promotion of the event? What can be done better next time?

Or was this a more focused event designed to attract spiritual seekers and get them signed up for seeker small groups? If so, how many seekers were there, and how many took the step of joining a group? Was it what you hoped for? What can you celebrate? What can you learn from and improve?

If it was an evangelistic, draw-the-net event designed to lead people to trust in Christ, how many actually did so? We know the Holy Spirit must do his work and draw people to the point of commitment, but did you do everything you could to produce the right environment for him to work? Did you pray for and seek his guidance in the planning of the event? Did you design it in a way that would help people relax and open up to the message? Did you clearly communicate the gospel message? Did you do everything in your power to promote the event and get the right people there?

It's vital that we measure the actual results, compare them to our original goals, and then determine how we can do better next time.

A final thought on evaluation: Beware of what I call the "Great Evangelical Rationalization." This is what comes out of someone's mouth when he or she is trying to make the team feel better about an unsuccessful outreach effort. Everybody knows the event didn't live up to the expectations you had for it. But rather than just admitting problems and resolving to make changes next time, someone comes out with, "Well, at least one person came to Christ. This was hard work and it used up a lot of time and resources — but it was all worth it for that one soul!"

The last line is the capper: "It was all worth it for that one soul." Who wants to dispute that? Who wants to weigh the value of a life that has been impacted for all eternity, but then blurt out that the event was really a misfire? That's pretty hard to do. But if the goal was to lead many to Christ and only one was reached, it must be done.

The Great Evangelical Rationalization has stopped countless evaluation sessions dead in their tracks. The problem is that it focuses the group on the wrong question. The soul of a person is of immeasurable worth, to be sure, but the question is not how much a soul is worth! The question ought to be, "What could we have done to have reached many more people?" And, "What could we do next time that might reach five or fifty people — or even five hundred — instead of just one?" Or, if it was more of an introductory event, "What could have been done to have exposed more people to the church?" Or, "What might have better helped more seekers to take the next step in their spiritual journeys?" These are the kinds of questions that will yield constructive conversations among your team and, eventually, greater results.

So the next time someone in the group starts to kill the evaluation time with an eloquent rendition of the Great Evangelical Rationalization, look him or her in the eye and say, "Yes, that's a good point. Before we get too caught up in figuring out how we can improve next time, let's acknowledge what God did this time for this precious person. But then, after praying and thanking God, I think we should explore some ideas for what we can do next time around that might help us reach a lot more of this person's friends too."

It'll take some courage, but make sure your team learns from the past and applies the lessons in the future. And then watch God work!

## 10. Permeate the Entire Process with Prayer

It's hard to know where to place prayer in a list like this. It could be listed as a parallel point to every other idea, as well as to every stage in the 6-Stage Process. But regardless of where it is or is not mentioned, please realize how important it is to every part and at every stage. *Prayer needs to permeate the entire process.*

Individually and as a team, you should pray during the idea-generation phase, asking God to give you insights into where he is already at work, so you can align your efforts with his. Then in the planning and promotion phase, ask God for guidance on how to best get the word out, and pray for his blessing on those efforts. And at the actual ministry event, ask God to draw the right people to attend, and give them open hearts to hear and embrace his message. Ask him to protect every aspect of the meeting and to use it to change lives and build his kingdom. Finally, when your ministry event is over, thank God for the work he has accomplished, and ask him to continue what he has begun to do in the lives of those who were there.

To illustrate, when I was considering holding the debate on "Atheism vs. Christianity," I remember seeking God for wisdom and guidance as diligently as I've ever sought him. I knew that if we did this event, it would draw a lot of attention as well as scrutiny. The last thing I wanted to do was to pull the trigger presumptuously, and then inform God that I was counting on him to come through for us. The image kept coming to my mind of Satan tempting Jesus to throw himself down from the temple and trust God to protect him on the way down. Jesus answered him, "Do not put the Lord your God to the test" (Luke 4:12).

I was so concerned that I delayed the decision to host the event for about two weeks. During this time I prayed alone and with informed friends, and I sought counsel from a number of older and wiser Christians. After getting a lot of green lights, I finally said yes and put the plan into motion, but with a deep sense of dependency on God. For the weeks that followed, right up to the event itself, the team and I prayed fervently for God's protection and blessing on the event.

During the debate, members of the prayer team sat alone in a room, watching by video monitor, asking God to let his truth prevail, to draw seekers to himself, and to build up the confidence of the believers who were there. By divine coincidence, the only video room left after the crowd overflowed into all of the other rooms was one directly below the stage in our main auditorium, where the debate was taking place. As Lee Strobel now describes it, "We had a secret weapon under that stage that the atheist never knew about!"

"So, *did* God come through?" you ask? Yes, he did, in amazing ways (as you can see on the video![9]). He protected and anointed every aspect of what happened that night—other than the words of the man defending atheism!

The potential in outreach events is huge—but only if we are led by God and empowered through submissive, persistent prayer.

## GETTING OFF THE GROUND

You now have the framework and personnel in place to unleash an array of outreach activities—and given the critical needs in the culture we're trying to reach, there is no better time to put it all into action than right now. But one question remains: What kinds of outreach ministries and events should you initiate?

Several clues can help you answer that question. First, what are the needs of the people you'd like to reach? What kinds of ministries and events would they relate to and be willing to attend? Second, prayerfully seek God's direction for where you should expend your efforts. Survey the needs and opportunities you see, and ask him to guide you whether to focus on one of those or to seek new ones. Pray that he'll give you and your team a passion for building ministries and doing outreach exactly where he wants you to work.

## UNLEASHING THE TEAM ACCORDING TO EVANGELISM STYLES

Another important clue to our criteria list is to look at what would best fit your personal style of evangelism.[10]

When you explore your own natural outreach inclinations, you'll likely find that they flow along the lines of your evangelism style. So, rather than resisting your God-given design, consider where it might match up with some of the needs in your community. If God has molded you into *who* you are today, and if he has led you to be *where* you are today, then he has likely placed you near ministry opportunities that are crying out for what you can offer.

Once I discovered my own style of evangelism, I immediately began to see needs around me that I was designed by God to address. Since I have the Intellectual Style, these needs were naturally of an intellectual nature. That's why if you look back over the pages of this book you'll notice that I've shared a number of stories about people with questions, and I've talked about seminars and debates designed to help people with spiritual doubts. Even the book's opening story was about a man with serious objections. I can't help myself! It's who God made me to be, and he has provided me with opportunities to express this approach, answer people's questions, and use my evangelism style to lead them toward the cross of Christ. When I have the chance to work within this design, I'm naturally motivated and energized. And when I get around others who have this same style, conversations flow, ideas fly, arguments abound, and we have a ball!

Now, I fully understand that five out of six readers are scratching their heads right now. You're thinking, *You "have a ball" talking about all that heady, intellectual stuff? Really? What's wrong with you?* Well, apparently you have a different evangelism style! You have one of the other five, or a combination of two or three of them—or maybe a new one we haven't discovered yet. But if I were discussing your particular approach right now, your heart would be pumping fast too.

What can we learn from this? That finding our own style of evangelism has value way beyond Stage 4, where we train everybody in the church to communicate their faith in ways that fit them. It goes beyond Stage 5 as well, where we can help everyone in the Frontline ministry develop and grow within their natural style. It also has powerful implications for Stage 6, where we can build entire outreach ministries and events around these six styles. When we do this, we're going to have a lot of high-octane ministry going on, because we'll be giving people permission, tools, and platforms to do what they were made by God to do.

One time we had everybody at a Frontline meeting retake the styles questionnaire from session two of the *Becoming a Contagious Christian* course, just to confirm what their dominant style was. Then we had them move to designated parts of the room where they could interact with others who share their style. This gave them the chance to find their similarities and then to compare and contrast these similarities to the traits of the people in the other groups. It also helped them identify which team members, by virtue of their different styles, might make good partners for them in reaching out to non-Christians in their own communities. For example, Interpersonal Style evangelists realized they could team up with Intellectual Style members to reach their friends or neighbors who are asking tough questions.

After a time of interacting within these six groups and letting them grapple with some questions we'd given them to discuss, each group's spokesperson shared his or her group's answers with the whole team. We had fun with the first one: "Why is your style the most important of the six?" The second question was: "How is your style sometimes misunderstood?" And the third was: "Where do you think your style can work most effectively?"

After each group gave their responses, Garry Poole and I had the chance to encourage and challenge the people with that particular style and to give them ideas for growing in their approach. This also gave us the opportunity to highlight ministries and events throughout the church where we needed their specific contributions.

At the end we asked team members to turn in a card listing their name and top two evangelism styles so we could enter that information into our church database. Since that time I've also incorporated this idea into the updated *Becoming a Contagious Christian* course, so every church can track which members have which styles. That way whenever you need people to serve in a particular outreach area, you can quickly pinpoint and talk to the people who would best fit it. And since there really is a fit, you'll discover that they *want* to know about the opportunity as much as you want to find people to help!

## A MULTISTYLED OUTREACH MODEL

Corinth Reformed Church, in Byron Center, Michigan, took this a step further and structured their entire evangelism team around the styles of evangelism. Kevin Harney[11], the church's senior pastor at the time, describes what they did:

> We repeatedly offered the *Becoming a Contagious Christian* course, with the goal of equipping all of our church members. As we did this, we helped each of them discover their primary evangelism style. We also pulled together all of those who have a heart for being part of our evangelism ministry and started Frontline.
>
> Next, we identified a lead person for each of the styles of evangelism. Each of these men and women work under our main evangelism leader. With great intentionality, they each gather others who have the same style and forge a team of people who are ready to go out and do evangelism the way God wired them up to do so. They lift up the value of that style, plan events, and strategize ways to have maximum kingdom impact using their particular approach.
>
> We found that when you gather a group of people around each of the styles of evangelism and ask them to dream, strategize, and pray, unbelievable energy and enthusiasm are generated.

They want to get up out of their chairs, leave the room, and take action—right now!

We discovered that by developing our team intentionally around the varied styles of evangelism, we've grown increasingly focused in how we can plan events that will reach our community and world for Christ.

## MULTIPLE TOOLS IN THE TOOLBOX

It's exciting to know that the six styles of evangelism provide us with six powerful conduits through which high-impact ministry can flow. Let me end this chapter and this discussion of Stage 6 with a challenge and an idea.

The challenge is this: Don't unnecessarily limit your church's outreach to just one or two particular ministries or events—and don't think you need to quit one so you can start another. Often churches get far too linear in their thinking and say things like, "We used to have a visitation team, but we disbanded that and started an evangelistic small group ministry instead." Really? Is there a law against multiple approaches? It's like saying, "I went to the hardware store and bought a screwdriver, so I came back home and threw away my hammer!" Why? Doesn't it take multiple tools to accomplish multiple tasks? Well let me declare right now that I'm an advocate of using complete toolboxes filled with a variety of tools for a variety of important purposes! That's why Stage 6 says we want to "Unleash an *Array* of Outreach Ministries and Events"—and not just one or two.

The idea? Follow Kevin Harney's lead and appoint leaders over each of the evangelism styles areas, and then over time unleash a whole boatload of high-impact outreach efforts. Invent new ones where needed, but don't waste time reinventing wheels where there are already proven models you can readily adopt and use!

For example, consider deploying your Direct Style evangelists into an Evangelism Explosion, Continuing Witness Training (CWT), or FAITH program that harnesses them to impact the community in direct ways. Another tool that teaches an effective direct approach is Kirk Cameron and Ray Comfort's *The Way of the Master*.

Put your Intellectual Style folks into action leading classes and seminars on various religions, cults, and secular challenges to the faith. The ones who develop real expertise in some area of study can become part of a team of apologetics consultants available to teach and coach church members, or to talk to spiritual seekers after church services.

Encourage your Testimonial Style people to write out and polish their stories to be used where appropriate in church services and outreach events—as well as to spice up the bulletin and church website (two arenas in most churches that definitely could stand to be spiced up with some interesting stories).

Members with the Interpersonal Style often make great leaders of seeker small groups or Alpha group meetings. Or partner with them to open and staff a "hospitality room" or "welcome center" for visitors to stop by after church services. Other ministries for this style might be to launch a supper club ministry (I'm not sure how it works, but these folks will figure it out!) or a business lunch outreach.

Invitational Style people can help shape communication tools that the rest of the church can use to invite their friends and neighbors to key outreach services or ministry events—including the sixth week of the churchwide *Contagious Campaign*, designed to present the gospel to visitors. And these folks can set the pace by filling their vans or SUVs with the people they're bringing.

And, finally, the Serving Style people can launch and serve in their own array of food pantries, homeless shelters, car repair ministries, hospital visitation teams, and so on—serving multiple needs while pointing to the love and care of the one true God who motivates them.

In sum: the *sky* is not even the limit! Unleash your church to reach out to the community in a variety of ways, and encourage and support them as God uses them all to lead many into the church and, ultimately, into a relationship with Christ.

## STAGE 6: KEY IDEA

*Unleash an array of high-impact outreach ministries and events.*

Be wise in the way you act toward outsiders; make the most of every opportunity. (Colossians 4:5)

# TO CONSIDER AND DISCUSS

1. Based on needs or opportunities you see in your community, what are some outreach ministries or events you might want to start in your church?

2. Based on your own style of evangelism, is there a ministry or outreach event that you'd be especially excited about launching?

3. What are some ideas for forming clear communications and alliances between your evangelism leadership (or the Frontline team, if you've already begun one) and all of the other ministries in your church?

4. Choose a specific upcoming churchwide outreach opportunity and discuss how you might apply the ten principles discussed in this chapter.

5. Which of the ten principles tends to get overlooked by your team? What can you do to make sure this "missing link" is addressed in the future?

6. What can you do to increase the practice of prayer in every stage of the 6-Stage Process?

# CONTAGIOUS VISION

We've seen the critical need for establishing and expressing our evangelistic mission (Part 1). We've unpacked the 6-Stage Process for putting this mission into action and increasing our church's overall evangelistic impact (Part 2). The elements seem to be in place. What's left to discuss in Part 3?

Two things: *courage* and *action*.

*Courage*—to boldly and unapologetically communicate the message of the cross of Christ. We live in a culture—in the world and sometimes even in the church—where we're pressured to tone down what we say about biblical topics such as sin, judgment, and hell. There's a powerful pull—one that can affect leaders of all kinds of churches—toward substituting uplifting stories and positive platitudes for the pride-shattering but eternity-altering truths of the gospel. So chapter eight reminds us that if we do everything else right but fail on this one, we've failed entirely. We must faithfully and courageously preach the gospel message, remembering that it is today and always "the power of God for the salvation of everyone who believes."

*Action*—which is the outward expression of courage. We must go beyond just understanding the evangelistic needs and opportunities that surround us. We must begin taking the steps, making the changes, and initiating the activities necessary to reach more and more lost people for Christ. Chapter nine pulls together all of the principles in this book, adds a few final thoughts, and urges us to move forward confidently in God's power in order to increasingly become a contagious church.

# CHAPTER EIGHT

# COMMUNICATING THE GOSPEL WITHOUT COMPROMISE

IT WAS BOLD, HARD-HITTING, AND direct—even borderline dangerous. It certainly wouldn't get a favorable review in *The Journal of Political Correctness.*

The setting: *Easter Sunday.* Many visitors were present, including a number of spiritual seekers and skeptics. The music was upbeat and celebratory. The people in the seats were mostly joyful, smiling, and wearing their "Sunday best"—clothes that in many cases hadn't been out of the closet since, well, last Easter. Families were sitting together ready to enjoy a pleasant church service and then go out for a nice brunch. The sun was even shining!

Enter the pastor. He walked quietly to the podium looking a tad somber. He welcomed the crowd, said a short prayer, and then, after very brief introduction, launched into his sermon: "I want to start right out by saying this: if Jesus was who he said he was and if he really did come back from the dead, then biblical Christianity is true and every other religion in the world is false!"

*Start with this?* And then what—really get serious?

What was this pastor thinking? Did he get up on the wrong side of the bed? Did he have too much caffeine in his Starbucks that morning—or maybe not enough? Didn't he realize that it was Easter Sunday—the day everybody comes to church to feel good?

If we could have gotten inside of his head we would have understood what he was thinking—and agreed with it! He was standing in front of these people with an acute awareness that some of them didn't know God and were therefore guilty before him, but fooling themselves with religious games and wishful thinking. He knew that, apart from a strong spiritual intervention, they faced a Christless eternity in a very real place called hell. He was telling himself, "This is my one shot for the entire year—and maybe my one shot ever—to jolt some of these people out of spiritual complacency, fuzzy thinking, and false hopes and get them focused on the realities of where they stand before a just and holy God." He was simply trying to honor the biblical command of 2 Timothy 4:2–5 (TNIV) that says:

> Preach the Word; be prepared in season and out of season; correct, rebuke and encourage—with great patience and careful instruction. For the time will come when people will not put up with sound doctrine. Instead, to suit their own desires, they will gather around them a great number of teachers to say what their itching ears want to hear. They will turn their ears away from the truth and turn aside to myths. But you, keep your head in all situations, endure hardship, do the work of an evangelist.

## THE EVANGELISTIC ESSENTIAL

We've talked about many things related to becoming effective evangelistic churches. We've looked at how the evangelism priority must permeate our mission. We've examined the 6-Stage Process for raising and expressing this priority. We've fleshed out the practical expression of this process by describing various outreach ministries and events to consider and use. I'm convinced—and I trust you are too—that these are all important elements for attaining our goal and reaching more and more lost people in our communities.

But let's be very clear: None of these plans or approaches will make our churches truly contagious if the core message we're proclaiming—at both the personal and public levels—is not the uncompromised gospel of Jesus Christ and his blood shed to pay for our sins.

If you think it takes a modern message to reach modern people, I think you're wrong. The gospel message is unchanging and it applies to all people in all places at all times. The apostle Paul said it well in Romans 1:16: "I am not ashamed of the gospel, because it is the power of God for the salvation of everyone who believes: first for the Jew, then for the Gentile."

Now, it may take a modern *method* to effectively communicate the age-old gospel message. Paul said in 1 Corinthians 9:22 (NRSV), "I have become all things to all people, that I might by all means save some." But then he quickly followed up in the next verse with words that affirm that his "becoming all things" is always and unswervingly subservient to proclaiming God's unchanging message. He said, "I do it all for the sake of the gospel, so that I may share in its blessings."

We, like Paul, must be cautious in how we apply this relevancy principle, always making sure our desire to relate to people is never allowed to distort or alter our biblical message. As I've written previously, "Contagious churches have learned that they must communicate *to* their culture without compromising *with* their culture. They know that if the message of the cross of Christ is ever diluted or hidden, then the battle has already been lost. What good is it to speak the language of secular people if we lose our message in the process?"[1]

Paul made clear his own commitment to proclaim the unaltered gospel message in 1 Corinthians 2:2: "I resolved to know nothing while I was with you except Jesus Christ and him crucified." He intentionally focused on that simple yet central truth, refusing to add or subtract any elements. Under the guidance of the Holy Spirit, he also challenged us to follow his example: "But even if we or an angel from heaven should preach a gospel other than the one we preached to you, let him be eternally condemned! As we have already said, so now I say again: If anybody is preaching to you a gospel other than what you accepted, let him be eternally condemned!" (Galatians 1:8–9).

This is a stern warning about a vitally important issue. Scripture does not mince words for anyone who claims to be a teacher of the gospel but who meddles with the message. If you or your church are ever tempted to modify or soften this message—even a little—in the hopes of gaining acceptance and admiration from an unbelieving audience, think again. To do so would be to forget the mission Jesus gave us, and to dilute the message that has the power to save.

After Paul gave the admonition in Galatians 1:8–9, he concluded in verse 10 with these strong words: "Am I now trying to win the approval of men, or of God? Or am I trying to please men? If I were trying to please men, I would not be a servant of Christ."

We have a mandate to please God alone by communicating the pure gospel message alone—whether people like it or not. The ironic thing is that most real seekers are looking for a believer who has the courage to look them in the eye and tell them the truth about their spiritual predicament—and then show them the way to the One who can help them. And even when people don't want to hear about the cross—as some won't—we need to gently but clearly present Christ anyway, asking him to use our efforts, bless his message, and draw people to himself. Many times our listeners will be initially offended by the gospel; but then as they mull over its seemingly audacious claims, and as the Holy Spirit convicts them of sin and draws them to the truth, they'll end up trusting in Christ.

## SHORING UP YOUR CONFIDENCE

### Fresh Experience

Perhaps you like the sound of what I'm saying but, truth be told, lack confidence in the power of the gospel. Maybe you need to spend some time around other ministries that God is really using in order to have your faith expanded. It might do you and your team a world of good to go across town or across the country to a church or conference where you can hear stories and see evidence of ongoing life change. You'll not only pick up practical ideas, but also gain a fresh hope and vision for the redemptive potential of your own church.

### Fresh Facts

Consider also the possibility that somewhere along the line your trust in the Bible has been shaken—perhaps because of the cynical words of a university teacher or even a seminary professor. Or maybe an articulate but skeptical friend threw challenges in your path you didn't know how to handle. It could have happened recently or many years ago, but if you've never risen to the challenge and done the work of finding answers, these things can daunt your faith and rob you of your confidence in the reliability of the Bible and the power of the gospel.

If this is your situation, I can relate! In college I took a philosophy class in which the teacher—an ordained Protestant minister—systematically assailed what he considered to be the Christian students' unsophisticated trust in "traditional theology" and "literal interpretations of the Bible." When these attacks come from eloquent and respected teachers with impressive credentials and a lot of letters behind their names, they're hard to deflect. You might keep a poker face and pretend your faith is unfazed, but it will very likely affect your conviction level when you later look a seeker or a congregation in the eye and try to tell them why they need to trust and follow Christ.

But remember this: smart people have been wrong before—including your seemingly wise old professor! And other smart people disagree with these smart people, and everybody can't be right! Truth can't be ascertained by adding up the number of professors or even pastors who take a certain stand. You have to do your homework for yourself. Get to the root issues. Listen to the arguments and be alert to the assumptions and biases. Read the defenses of the faith by some leading apologists. Pray for wisdom and for genuine answers as you study. Seek and you will find. And you'll feel your spiritual certainty climbing by the moment!

This is the process I had to go through in college. Along the way I found out that my skeptical professor had never read any of the powerful books that defend biblical orthodoxy. He was too busy perusing his liberal theology journals to trifle with teachers who might actually answer his objections. I began to read what he wouldn't and found penetrating answers to the challenges he'd been presenting. The more I studied, the higher my confidence level grew—to the point where I had much more faith in the truths of historic Christianity than I'd ever had before. In fact, I felt so emboldened that I went to the leaders of a local campus ministry and arranged to teach at two of their large group meetings. I wanted to share my discoveries with the other students whose theological cages had also been rattled.

What about you? Do you need to reinforce your foundation of facts and evidence? If so, do your homework. Really commit to it. For your own sake and the sake of those you influence, go after it with vigor. Read the books, have the conversations, go to the classes and seminars, and do everything necessary to bolster your faith. If you don't know where to start, try books such as *The Case for Christ*, *The Case for Faith*, and *The Case for the Real Jesus* by former skeptic Lee Strobel.[2] The apologetic classics *More Than a Carpenter* by Josh McDowell[3] and *Know Why You Believe* by Paul Little[4] also can be a tremendous help, though they're geared more to an entry level. Start there, and then go on to the more advanced works by thinkers like J. P. Moreland, William Lane Craig,

Gary Habermas, and Norman Geisler. Reading cover to cover the text-book by Geisler and William Nix, *A General Introduction to the Bible*,[5] did wonders for my faith during my era of questioning in college. The deeper you look into the basis of our Christian beliefs, the more confident you'll become.

### Fresh Faith

One principle for strengthening your trust in the Bible—often over-looked because of its simplicity—is to *read it regularly.* Doubts can easily creep in when we aren't staying in the Book and opening ourselves up to fresh shots of inspiration, insights, and instructions from the God who inspired it.

I don't want to be legalistic about it, but sometimes even as commit-ted Christians we need to be reminded that "faith comes by hearing, and hearing by the word of God" (Romans 10:17 NKJV). I need—and you need—to "let the word of Christ dwell in [us] richly" (Colossians 3:16). We need to become so saturated with the truths of Scripture that, over time, we gain "the mind of Christ" (1 Corinthians 2:16) and begin, as John MacArthur puts it, "to see the world through chapter and verse eyes." That's why my longtime friend and accountability partner, Brad Mitchell, and I have agreed to ask each other regularly if we're staying active in reading the Scriptures. We want to reinforce Bible reading as a habitual, lifelong pattern. Staying in the Book increases our spiritual confidence and courage, making us bolder in proclaiming its message to others.

## COMMUNICATE THE GOSPEL WITHOUT COMPROMISE

With our confidence levels strengthened, how can we communicate the uncompromised message of Christ in ways that are clear and that really connect with people who live on the far side of the secular spectrum? Well, we've talked about it, and now I want to present an example of it. One of the best ways to learn how to communicate the message to non-Christians clearly is to see it done well.

The following is a message called "The Core Idea," delivered by Bill Hybels at one of Willow Creek's weekend services, designed to teach believers and to reach spiritual seekers.[6] I hope you'll be encouraged by its content and inspired by its approach to communicating a complex set of biblical truths in a relevant fashion and at a clear, introductory level.

Whenever I'm learning something new, I usually feel a bit confused until I can wrap my arms around the core idea of whatever the subject is. But once I get that idea under my belt, I can usually relax and enjoy the learning process.

When I was sixteen and first taking flying lessons, I remember sitting in a side room of a hangar in Kalamazoo, Michigan, wondering if I was the only person in the class who didn't understand how airplanes stay in the air. I was anxious about this until the instructor took out a flip chart and started drawing some diagrams. He said the twin enemies of flight are *gravity* and *drag*. Gravity pulls the plane down, and drag holds the plane back. "But," he said, "a properly designed airframe and wing and a properly powered engine will enable a plane to defeat those enemies with two things called *lift* and *speed*."

Once I saw that, I got it: *the core idea of flight.* Then I was able to settle in and enjoy the rest of the flight training. I've been flying ever since, and even to this day I operate with that core idea in mind.

The same is true in academics. If you're studying political science in college and you hear terms being tossed about like *fascism*, *socialism*, *communism*, and *democracy*, you probably feel nervous until an instructor boils down each complicated governing process to just a core idea. Then you say, "Oh, that's not all that complicated. I get it!"

Now, today, before you walk out of this place, it's my goal that you will understand the core idea of Christianity. I really hope that you walk out the door with the full assurance that you get it—that you understand the basic idea of what Christianity is all about.

For some of you, this is going to be review. It will reinforce what you already know, and that's a good thing. For others, this is going to be clarifying. The haze is going to dissipate somewhat and you're going to see the core idea with new sharpness and definition. And for still others, this is going to hit you like a bolt of lightning. You've never heard Christianity boiled down to its very core in terms you could understand. Today might just change everything in your life now and in your whole eternity.

To get us headed in that direction, have you heard about the videotape that was discovered of Richard Speck? He's the guy who assaulted and murdered eight young Chicago nurses in 1966. This was one of the first mass murders of my generation, and it traumatized the entire city of Chicago for months. Every day, the cry went out for Richard Speck to pay for his crime. I remember the outrage all over the city.

Well, he was tried and convicted. And then he was locked away in Stateville Prison, near Joliet, for eight consecutive life sentences. So that was that! Then he died in 1991.

But recently a video was released showing how Richard Speck spent the final years of his life living like a little king in prison. He had free access to drugs and alcohol whenever he wanted it. He had numerous homosexual lovers who would come in and out of his cell. He had carved out a country club kind of life in Stateville Prison.

But it was all recorded on videotape and got into the hands of a news reporter, and it's been a big deal. People are outraged all over again. Why? Because it seems like he didn't make appropriate payment for his crime. And there's just this thing about society—it can't put a crime behind it until there has been an appropriate payment made.

*Appropriate payment.* Hold on to that concept. In fact, let's call it *atonement*—because it's the same concept, essentially. Atonement is satisfying the demands of justice when a crime has been committed. And we all carry an intuitive understanding of this notion in our heads.

So do you have the idea of atonement now? It's satisfying the demands of justice when a crime has been committed.

The second half of the core idea of Christianity comes out of another word we're quite familiar with—*substitution*. We use this a lot in our culture. It's whoever comes into the basketball game when Dennis Rodman gets kicked out!

*Substitute.* Taking the place of another. I think we understand this. Remember what we used to do to substitute teachers? I still carry a little guilt about that!

Now put those two words together. *Substitutionary atonement*—it's somebody taking the place of someone else and satisfying the demands of justice when a crime has been committed.

I want to clarify this concept further by taking you for a little walk through the Bible and showing you how this pertains to Christianity and to your life. We're going to start all the way back in the book of Genesis. Shortly after God created Adam and Eve, he said to them, "I've breathed life into you. You can make all kinds of decisions, you're smart, and I love you. We'll commune together, and it's going to be a wonderful experience. But I am a holy and just God. If you start sinning and violating my laws and shaking your fist at me,

I've got to let you know something: This wonderful gift of life that I breathed into you is going to come to a screeching halt. You're going to die."

He made it all very clear. But as you know, Adam and Eve bought into a lie from the Evil One and flagrantly disobeyed God. So now all of creation holds its breath wondering, What is God going to do? Will he strike them dead on the spot for their rebellion? Or maybe the whole death warning was just a hoax and God's going to wink and say, "Just kidding! Apple eating is hardly a crime deserving capital punishment. Boys will be boys; girls will be girls. No problem. I'm going to walk away from this one."

What's going to happen? Do you remember what God does? He doesn't strike them dead on the spot, but he doesn't wink and walk away either.

First, he explains that the whole universe is going to be sin-tainted because of what they did. They've opened the door, and now sin is in the world. Human labor is going to be affected, childbearing is going to be painful, human relationships will be complicated by ego, and human bodies will grow old and eventually die.

And God explains that people who continue to live in patterns of rebellion and resistiveness to him will pay. They'll atone for their crimes against God in this life and all throughout eternity in hell.

Sin is a serious thing. But at the end of God's explanation of the consequences of sin, we read in Genesis 3:21 that God does something that must have knocked the wind out of Adam and Eve, who were cowering in shame and guilt for what they had done. The text says that God covered their shame and nakedness with an animal skin. Most people just read right over that and say, "Okay, no big deal." But it *is* a big deal. I think it's our first glimpse of the arrangement that God is designing to provide sinners with an alternative way to have their sins atoned for.

Picture again God's dilemma. He's the absolutely holy and righteous God. He cannot allow sin to go unatoned for—it's got to be paid for. At the same time, he's a tender, loving God whose heart has been captured by these two people and all the others who will follow. The thought of Adam and Eve atoning for their own sins for the rest of their lives and in eternity in hell just breaks the heart of God. It moves him to take upon himself the responsibility for providing an alternative way that sin can be legitimately paid for, without the sinner having to spend an eternity atoning for his own sin, and without God's holiness being compromised.

So look what God does—all the way back in the garden of Eden. He takes an animal—an innocent animal—and he kills it. Can you imagine Adam and Eve gasping in horror as they see death for the very first time? They hear the screech of the animal that's being killed. They see its awkward movements in its death throes. There's the bleating, the wrenching, the quivering, and then the stillness. And then God takes the skin of the animal and covers the shame and guilt and nakedness of Adam and Eve as if to say, "In order for your sinfulness to be covered, in order for your wrongdoings to be atoned for, an innocent party is going to have to bear the penalty that was rightfully yours."

And, friends, this was kind of a sneak preview. It was the beginning of the playing out of this idea of substitutionary atonement—the arrangement by God for an innocent party to stand in the place of the sinner and absorb the penalty due to that sinner, thereby satisfying the demands of justice. And the guilty party, then, is set free.

Later on in the history of God's people, we read the story of the exodus. Remember that? You've seen it on old TV movies! God's people, the Israelites, have become a faithless people, and they're being held captive by the Egyptians, who are slowly working them to death. The Egyptians are sinning against the Israelites, and the Israelites are sinning against each other and against the Egyptians—and the whole thing turns into a colossal, sinful mess.

This pushes God's patience to the breaking point. Scripture shows us that God is slow to anger; but if you push him long enough, his righteous wrath finally kicks in. That's what happens in this situation. God says, "Enough is enough!" God announces to all of the Israelites and the Egyptians that he's going to bring judgment. He's going to bring it to bear on everyone for their sin. He announces that an angel of death is going to circulate on a given night and take the life of every firstborn son in every household in the land. The wages of sin is death. There would be no exceptions.

But, God adds—almost as a P.S.—"I will offer one option. I will make one provision for any interested party. Anyone who gets an unblemished, prize-of-the-herd male lamb and slaughters it, sheds its blood, and sprinkles a bit of the blood over the doorframe of the front of the house—the angel of death, on that appointed night, will honor the blood of that lamb and pass over that house. The eldest son in that house will not be killed." God says, "That's my arrangement. So all of you can decide—what are you going to do on that given night?"

Well, as it happens, most people just ignore the whole thing. They say, "I don't think God's going to bring judgment. I don't think he's that kind of God. I think we can steamroll right over him and live however we want, and he's not going to lift a finger."

But there were a few people who decided otherwise. They said, "You know, I think if God is God, he is loving *and* just and holy. I think from time to time he'll bring judgment." So they go out and get the lamb.

I imagine a fifteen-year-old kid watching his dad search around in the herd. He finds the best lamb and he's just lifting the knife to kill it when his fifteen-year-old says, "Hey, Dad! What are you doing killing our prize lamb? What did the lamb do?" only to have the father respond, "Well, son, it's the lamb or you. It's atonement time. Sin is going to be paid for tonight. A holy God has said, 'Enough is enough.' It's the lamb or you."

We read that the next day every household that had offered up an innocent lamb and sprinkled the blood on the doorframe was spared the judgment. The lamb died, and the sons went free. But the households that didn't offer up the lamb paid with the life of the firstborn child.

Sin is serious. And when it's atonement time, sin gets paid for.

Do you see the substitutionary atonement principle in the story of the exodus? An innocent lamb takes the hit for the wrongdoing of others, and guilty parties go free.

Later on in the Old Testament, you see the sacrificial system. It foreshadows the substitutionary atonement idea as well. Whenever a person sinned grievously, an animal sacrifice would be made; an innocent lamb would be slain. Only after the death of the lamb would the priest give the guilty sinner the assurance that his or her sin had been atoned for, and then that person could go free.

Then a prophet named Isaiah announces something that makes people's heads spin and hearts stop. In one of his prophecies he says: "But he was wounded for our transgressions, he was bruised for our iniquities.... And the Lord will lay on him the iniquity of us all." People didn't know how to handle this prophecy because it sure sounded as though someday, somewhere, God was going to send a human sacrifice to make an ultimate atonement for the sins of the world.

And then, later on, Jesus is born. And he's born amid all of the miraculous circumstances of his birth. He grows up, and there are all of these indications that he's God's Son.

When he's about thirty years old, he goes out one day to where another prophet is preaching. This guy's name is John the Baptist, and a large crowd of people is listening to him. Jesus stands on the fringe of the crowd; and John the Baptist sees him, stops preaching, and says, "Look, everybody!" And he points right at Jesus and says, "Behold, the Lamb of God who takes away the sin of the world."

Here he is, John was saying, the one we've all been thinking about, the one Isaiah prophesied was coming. He's God's ultimate provision for atonement. He's the unblemished prize lamb that will be offered as the ultimate substitute for sin. He's the one that tens of thousands of sacrificial lambs have been foreshadowing all these years.

The people strained to understand, just like many of you who are seekers are straining to understand what I'm saying right now. You're thinking, *Can it be so? How does it all fit together?*

When Jesus began his teaching ministry, he began to refer to himself in these sacrificial terms. He'd give a great talk and people would be applauding. Then he'd add, "But you've got to know something. Not too long from now, I'm going to be sacrificed for all of your sins." And the people said, "No, no, no!"

Then he'd teach another message, and people would go, "Oh, that's great. We love to hear you preach, Jesus." Then he would say, "I'm going to lay down my life for you," and "I am the Lamb of God who's going to take away the sin of the world." And I'm telling you, people just couldn't take it in.

But, sure enough, after leading a sinless, unblemished life, he was arrested and falsely convicted. He was beaten and battered. All the saints and angels in heaven looked on in horror as Jesus was nailed to a cross outside the city of Jerusalem. You think Adam and Eve cringed when they saw death for the first time? You think the fifteen-year-old boy at the time of the exodus got a little nauseated when he saw his father kill a lamb in the backyard? Imagine what was going on in heaven as Jesus, the innocent second member of the Trinity, slowly bled to death in front of a group of gawkers who—instead of bowing low to worship Jesus for what he was doing—were busy auctioning his robe to the highest bidder. You can bet there was some major cringing and crying going on in heaven when Jesus, the innocent Lamb of God, finally cried out, in effect, "It is finished! I have made atonement for the sins of the world." It just didn't seem right in heaven. The price seemed too high. Guilty sinners don't deserve a substitute like the one God provided. They ought to pay for their own sins.

And you know what? *We should! I* should because I'm the one who does them. *You* should because you're the one who does them. We're the foul-ups. We're the ones who know God's rules and break them. We're the ones who lie when we ought to tell the truth. We're the ones who hate when we ought to love. We're the ones who will hold back when we ought to give. We're the ones who put down when we ought to lift up. We are the ones who ought to include everybody. You know, all people matter to God. But some of us exclude some people for the sheer perverse pleasure of freezing them out of our circles. That's the kind of people we are. And we should atone for those kinds of crimes. I should, and you should.

But the Bible says, in those words you've heard since you were kids, "God so loved the world." You know, as holy, righteous, and just as God is, he has this thing about you. You matter to him. He knows your name. And whenever he thinks about you, his heart is moved with love. So the Bible tells us that God so loved the world that even though we ought to pay for our own sins, he sent his only begotten Son to stand in our place, to pay the penalty we should pay, to make substitutionary atonement for our sin.

Do you see the core idea of Christianity? Jesus Christ taking your place and mine, satisfying the demands of justice so guilty parties like you and me can go free. We can be forgiven and stand blameless before God on the merits of the Lamb of God who paid our price. What an idea! Every other religious system is based on a different core idea. Every other religious system establishes some kind of performance expectation. If you try hard and struggle and wrestle and give money and do all kinds of things, well, they say, you *might* raise your status enough to make it.

And people who do work at it hard often get proud and look down their self-righteous noses at those who aren't doing as well. And then people who don't do as well finally give up and say, "I might as well just take the heat for whatever I've gotta take the heat for."

Christianity is the only religion in the world whose core idea is based on substitutionary atonement—where guilty sinners go free on the merits of the provision God has made in Jesus, his Son, who pays the price on our behalf. It's an amazing thing. Some people have asked me, "How do you get so fired up and stay so fired up about Christianity?" I'm telling you, friends, this is the third time I've given this message this weekend. Whenever I talk about it, I can't get over it. There's nothing else like this in the world.

The Bible says that on the day of judgment, you're going to stand before a holy God, and there will be no argument whatsoever about whether or not you're a sinner. That's going to be the shortest discussion in history! You're going to know it right away.

In the early eighties, when I was a much younger man, I enjoyed playing park district football. I used to watch the Chicago Bears on television on Sunday afternoons, and I'd say, "You know, I could play with those guys. I really could! I could line up across from a couple of those guys and hold my own."

Then I was invited to be the chaplain for the Bears. I remember driving to Lake Forest for the first time to give my Bible study. I walked around a corner and saw Richard Dent. I was looking right at his navel! I looked at the size of all these guys, and I realized something: When you watch it from afar you can start thinking all kinds of strange thoughts that aren't true at all. But when you get up close, *reality* strikes!

From afar some of us say, "I'll hold my own when I stand before God. I've led a pretty good life." But stand five seconds in the blazing, brilliant holiness of God and you're going to say, "Oh my, I'm in trouble!" You're going to know who the Holy One is and who the sinner is that fast. On the judgment day the issue is not who's the sinner—the question is, who makes the atonement? Because in God's economy, sin will be paid for. It's just a question of who pays the tab.

The Bible says that between now and that day, you've got to make a decision. If you're going to take the hit and do your own atoning, then you'll do it forever—separated from God in a place called hell. It's your choice. But there's another option available to you: substitutionary atonement. It's Jesus Christ, out of love, saying, "I'll take your rap. I'll take the hit. I'll pay the penalty. And you, as a guilty party—on my merits—can be free, forgiven, adopted into God's family, blessed in love, and taken to heaven forever. Your choice!"

When you came in, in your bulletin there was a little card. Would you take that out for a minute? Everybody—not just seekers, because we're going to do something all together.

It says the core idea of Christianity is substitutionary atonement—Jesus Christ willingly shouldering the weight of my wrongdoing so that I could be set free. Now, here's what I'd like to have you do. I'd like to have you initial or write your name under that first blank where it says, "I understand the core idea of substitutionary atonement. *I get it.*" Also, where were you and when was it when you first got it?

I put, "August 1968." I was seventeen years old and at a Bible camp in southern Wisconsin when someone explained it to me. I said, *"I get it!"*

Now, if you don't get it yet, don't sign anything. Some of you might say, "Well, I get it right now. It's just been explained to me." Then put down today's date and "Willow Creek Community Church."

You can all talk about it afterward and show each other your cards and say, "That's where I was." And a lot of people, the last couple of hours, have put today's date or last night's date. It's a really exciting thing!

Here's the second part, equally important. The Bible says you can understand the core idea of Christianity and still wind up having to atone for your own sins for yourself in hell forever, because just *understanding* it is not enough. You have to, in humility and with a repentant spirit, say, "Not only do I understand it but I need it, I want it, and I reach out for it. I ask that what Jesus did be applied to my life and my sin. I place my trust solely in his substitutionary atonement for my hope of heaven."

The Bible says in John 1:12, "as many as *received* him...." You have to invite him into your life as your Savior and Friend. It says in Romans 10:13, "Whoever will *call on* the name of Lord...." You've got to do that.

So the second thing I'm asking you to do is to initial when and where that happened. When did you appropriate it? Just initial it if you've received the substitutionary atoning death of Christ. Put it down.

For me, "August 1968." About fifteen seconds after I got it, I said, "I need it!" I reached out for it. Jesus Christ's atoning work became real in my life, and I got off the treadmill of trying to earn my way to heaven. I said, "I can't earn it. Christ bought it for me. I receive it as a gift"—and it changed everything in my life.

When was it that this happened for you? If you're thinking, *Uh, oh—I don't know*, then it might be that you've never really appropriated the substitutionary work of Christ.

The great news is that you can get it squared away right now. If you're ready, just write down your initials to say, "I ask for Christ's atoning work to take effect in my life. I need it. I want it. I reach out for it by faith. I ask for it." And Christ will do that for you today. He *died* to do that for you.

For some of you this is all hitting you too fast. You're thinking, *Whoa, my head's spinning! I don't know what I'm doing here!* Then don't do anything right now. You've got to understand it. It's got to be genuine for it to be meaningful. Just keep coming back, keep seeking, keep asking questions. It might be a week from now, a month from now, or whenever. But some of you are ready right now. So let's just take a minute to write down when and where we received it, and then we'll close in prayer [pauses briefly].

Now, do you know what a lot of folks did the last couple of hours? Right after we closed in prayer, they showed their cards to each other. We had a fun time. We said, "If anyone said 'I got it and I appropriated it today,' then whoever they showed their card to had to buy them brunch!" And there's a whole lot of people saying, "Gladly— that would be the greatest thrill in the world!"

Before we close in prayer, I want to say one more thing. When you "get it"—the core idea—and Christ comes into your life, and if you have clear vision about life and eternity, it only seems appropriate that you would reorder your whole life around worshiping the God who provided you with an atonement substitution so you wouldn't have to pay. It only makes sense that you would proclaim this scandalous message of grace to almost everybody you know and that you'd spend large amounts of time figuring out ways to say thanks to God for what he's done. We're having a baptism service in a couple of weeks. For those of you who've done this recently, you can stand up here and give public witness to the fact that there was a time when *you* were going to have to atone, but now Christ has done this atoning work on your behalf. What a day of celebration that will be!

Let's pray:

Father, your love is so high, so deep, so wide, so pure, and so strong that you offered up your only Son as the substitutionary atonement for the likes of us guilty sinners. We ought to pay, but through Christ we've been set free. What a deal! What a God! What a Savior! What a faith!

I pray that as we dismiss today we will do so amazed by grace and committed to spreading it all over the world.

For Jesus' sake, Amen.

## BRINGING THE MESSAGE HOME

It has been said that if a preacher ever gives an audience the chance to misunderstand the message, people will grab that chance with both arms and run away with it! Nowhere is this truer than with the central message of the gospel. You can teach it, preach it, and teach it again — and some of the people who've heard it a hundred times will look you in the eye and say, "Well, I think I'm a pretty good person," or "I'm fairly confident that God will approve of my efforts and let me into heaven." You can explain God's free gift of grace, and they'll say, "Thanks ... I guess I'll have to work harder to earn it."

People just seem bent on not "getting it"! This was true in Jesus' day too. Look at Nicodemus's confusion as recorded in John 3 — a top religious leader and teacher, and yet he didn't get it. And, today, scores of people are part of the church crowds and considered to be real Christians, but their attitude says, "I've done the religious drill, been through the classes, said the right words, gotten the certificate. I'm OK and you're OK — so let's just accept each other, and live and let live!"

These people can often talk like they've got things spiritually figured out, at least when they're around the church, but in their heart of hearts many of them are not true followers of Christ. Paul warned in Titus 1:16 that there would be those who "claim to know God, but by their actions they deny him." In fact, a *Barna Report* said that, based on their team's surveys over the course of more than a decade, "close to half of the people who fill the pews on a typical Sunday are not Christians ... [and many are actually] atheists or agnostics."[7]

It's important to understand that these are not outside visitors. They're regular attenders who everyone thinks are on board — and as many as half of them still don't get it! They're churchgoing non-Christians who are often friendly and attractive people — and they certainly matter to

God—but they're snared in religious rituals and mistaken thinking that can actually inoculate them to the truth of the gospel. In pride, they keep living the way they've independently chosen to live, but they never bow before a holy God to acknowledge their sins or their desperate need for the Savior.

The important question for us is this: Have we warned them? Have we gone out of our way to make it clear that it's possible to be in a good church—like your church or mine—but not be in Christ? Have we urged our fellow members and attenders to examine themselves to see whether they're really in the faith (as we're urged in 2 Corinthians 13:5)? Have we loved them enough to risk offending them by proclaiming that we *all* need to humble ourselves and kneel, empty-handed and broken-hearted, at the foot of the cross of Jesus Christ—and that this is an attitude that marks his true followers throughout their lives?

In some church traditions this is a difficult message to deliver—everyone assumes that everybody is okay and they don't expect anyone to question that assumption. But these are the churches where the danger is the greatest and the need for clear warnings the highest.

I lived much of my life in an area where almost everyone was moderately "religious" and at least occasionally went to church. But from my observation, relatively few of them manifested changed hearts by being serious about following and serving Christ in their daily lives. And in many cases their churches reinforced the notion that they were alright the way they were.

This problem really hit home when a teenager was killed in an accident. He had been known for his reckless, ungodly lifestyle. As far as any of us could tell, his life showed no signs of a real relationship with Christ—and plenty of evidence to the contrary. Yet at his funeral the pastor reassured everyone that because this young man had been through their church's traditional rites of passage as a child, he was now in heaven enjoying God's presence and rewards. This, of course, encouraged friends and family members to breathe a sigh of relief—and prevented most of them from looking at their own hearts and lives to make certain they were really "in the faith." I can't help feeling that on that day an opportunity was missed for heaven—and all of hell laughed.

Paul warned Timothy (in 2 Timothy 1:7) about the danger of timidity. Evangelistic leadership is not for the faint of heart. It takes courage.

My greatest fear as a teacher of the gospel is not that I might offend someone, but that I would allow anyone I influence to keep on living with religious false securities—to let them go on, day after day, year after year, thinking everything is all right, only to later suffer the greatest shock and disappointment imaginable on the day of judgment. Jesus was very clear about this danger in Matthew 7:21–23 (TNIV): "Not everyone who says to me, 'Lord, Lord,' will enter the kingdom of heaven, but only those who do the will of my Father who is in heaven. Many will say to me on that day, 'Lord, Lord, did we not prophesy in your name, and in your name drive out demons and perform many miracles?' Then I will tell them plainly, 'I never knew you. Away from me, you evildoers!'"

Jesus said in no uncertain terms that people can be highly religious, say all the right things, address him in proper ways, engage in biblical activities and service—and still not know him or his salvation, and, as a result, end up separated from him for all of eternity.

So I urge you to have the evangelistic guts to ignore ecclesiastical correctness and break tradition in order to lovingly tell people the unadulterated truth—knowing that some will be offended while others will be redeemed. May God give you and those who serve with you the boldness and wisdom to do whatever it takes to overcome spiritual confusion, to confront sin, and to point people to Christ and his amazing grace, made available to all who will turn from their sins and follow him.

For many of us, evangelism needs to start in our own pews. Our churches need to become contagious *inside* before they'll ever become highly contagious *outside*.

## GETTING THE MESSAGE OUT

But we *do* need to spread this powerful message outside, as well—and when we do, it will have impact! As we near the end of this important chapter, let me share a few inspiring stories of impassioned Christians who took tenacious steps to communicate the gospel to others.

A friend took some days away from work, drove alone from Chicago to Iowa to pick up a former college classmate, and then spent almost a week touring with him all over the Midwest. Why? Because he wanted to carve out some uninterrupted time to explain to his friend the good news he'd discovered since they were in college together. The gospel was made clear, the Holy Spirit was at work, and on the last night of the trip his friend committed his life to Christ!

A woman I know was so concerned about the salvation of her ill and aging father that she made special arrangements to have her extremely busy pastor travel hundreds of miles, just so he could tell this man about Christ. She knew her pastor was effective in evangelism; and since she had not been able to break through to her dad, she decided to prevail upon her pastor to go and reinforce the message of God's love and forgiveness. I think that if this woman had decided she needed Billy Graham or Luis Palau to talk to her father next, she would have found a way to get them there! Her pastor went, and he helped her father move at least a few steps closer to the cross.

I have another friend, Wende, who as a first-year Christian shared the gospel with her father, Bob, and soon led him to Christ. Then the two of them began conspiring to reach another family member, "Uncle Lynn," who was aging and in poor health. They called him on the phone. They wrote to him. They sent him evangelistic books and recordings, as well as a copy of *The Journey*[8] Bible, which includes notes for spiritual seekers — something Lynn had never admitted to being! Bob took several trips to the East Coast to talk to Lynn about his need for Christ. They even arranged for a minister in Lynn's area to meet with him to remind him of God's message. The term *tenacious* seems tepid when I think of this father-daughter team. Bob later called to tell me he had taken yet another trip out east to visit Uncle Lynn — who had finally put his faith in Christ! Then, just two weeks later, Lynn passed away. He is in heaven today because, at least from a human standpoint, Bob and Wende knew the message, persisted in presenting it, and refused to give up.

Can you see the pattern in these stories? Ordinary Christians with unquenchable evangelistic spirits, clear on the gospel and confidently communicating it to the people around them — and lives and eternities impacted as a result. We need to become such people, inspiring fellow church members with our lives, and teaching them, so in turn they'll go and tell the message of God's love and truth to others.

## NOTHING BUT THE BLOOD

The gospel — the core idea of Christianity that says Christ died to pay for my sins and for yours — is needed by everybody, inside and outside the church walls. We have to proclaim this message clearly, without apology, and trust God to empower and apply it in ways that will change lives and build his church.

Let me end with the words of one of my favorite songs, "Nothing but the Blood." It expresses simply what we've been talking about—the truth the whole world needs to hear:

> What can wash away my sin? Nothing but the blood of Jesus;
> What can make me whole again? Nothing but the blood of Jesus.
> O! precious is the flow that makes me white as snow;
> No other fount I know, nothing but the blood of Jesus.
> This is all my hope and peace—nothing but the blood of Jesus;
> This is all my righteousness—nothing but the blood of Jesus.
> O! precious is the flow that makes me white as snow;
> No other fount I know, nothing but the blood of Jesus.

## TO CONSIDER AND DISCUSS

1. How clearly is the "core idea" of Christianity understood by your church's members? What steps, if any, might you take to deepen their grasp of the substitutionary atonement of Christ?

2. Have you ever had your "spiritual cage rattled" by challenges to your faith that you could not easily answer? What happened, and how did it affect you?

3. Have you ever really resolved those issues in your mind? Are there steps you need to take or is there any "homework" you need to do in order to restore your confidence in the Bible and the gospel message?

4. What are some steps you'll commit to and prioritize in order to strengthen the foundations of your faith?

5. Do the people in your congregation need more teaching in order to shore up their own confidence in the reliability of the Bible or the power of the gospel? If so, what can you do to remedy this situation?

# CHAPTER NINE

# CONTAGIOUS CHURCHES AND THE UNSTOPPABLE SPREAD OF THE CHRISTIAN FAITH

Broken relationships, broken families, broken promises, broken values, broken hearts, broken lives in a broken-down world....

In the midst of this mess, allow the local church to function as the church envisioned by Jesus Christ — a thriving, radiating center of Christian love reaching out in self-sacrificing concern toward the needs of contemporary women, men, and children. Let the church really be the church and watch it exert a supernatural power of attraction that will irresistibly draw our secular, community-starved contemporaries within its sphere of influence, bring them to Christ in the most natural manner, and integrate them into its life.

The best shot at evangelism is to encourage churches to become and to live as authentic, biblically defined communities so that the Lord himself can become their Master Evangelist.

Dr. Gilbert Bilezikian

What makes a church *truly* contagious? What kind of church does the Holy Spirit use to not only attract outsiders, but also to bring them to the point of trusting in Christ and then enfold them into the life of God's family? As I'm sure you're aware, it's more than just an *evangelistic* church! We've focused on evangelistic strategy and activity, both of which play the vital role of helping us make connections, open doors, and expose people to the truth of the gospel.

But once these people show up, they need to experience a living, vibrant, biblically functioning church — the kind that genuinely honors and worships God, teaches and submits to his Word, is faithful in prayer, experiences and extends authentic community, deals forthrightly with problems and conflicts, and expresses selfless love and service to people inside and outside its four walls.

It's this kind of combination that we see in the highly contagious church of Acts 2:42 – 47:

> They devoted themselves to the apostles' teaching and to the fellowship, to the breaking of bread and to prayer. Everyone was filled with awe, and many wonders and miraculous signs were done by the apostles. All the believers were together and had everything in common. Selling their possessions and goods, they gave to anyone as he had need. Every day they continued to meet together in the temple courts. They broke bread in their homes and ate together with glad and sincere hearts, praising God and enjoying the favor of all the people. And the Lord added to their number daily those who were being saved.

## A DISPROPORTIONATE INVESTMENT IN EVANGELISM

The early church had all of the right elements, and it set the original Spirit-inspired standard that we should all strive for in our own churches. It's this biblical mix that makes the church an absolute magnet to anyone who has even an ounce of spiritual openness and receptivity. So it's important in our effort to become a contagious church that we pay attention to the broader issue of church *health* and not focus on our outreach mission alone.

That said, let's not miss the fact that the Acts 2 church had *an extraordinary commitment to outreach*. It had been born out of evangelism, as recorded in the verses immediately preceding the Acts 2:42 – 47 passage regarding the amazing events of the day of Pentecost, and evangelism was its top priority. This can be clearly seen in the next couple of chapters, where Peter and John healed a man and then used the platform this provided to proclaim the gospel (Acts 3:11 – 26). When this led to their detainment by the authorities, they again made the most of the situation and presented the message of Christ to the people detaining them (Acts 4:8–12). Then, after being given a stern warning to stop preaching, they were released. The church's response to all of this? They prayed "Now, Lord, consider their threats and enable your servants to speak your word with great boldness ... and they were all filled with the Holy Spirit and *spoke the word of God boldly*" (Acts 4:29–31, emphasis mine).

And that was just the beginning! After Stephen, one of the church's leaders, was put to death as a follower of Christ, "a great persecution broke out against the church in Jerusalem, and all except the apostles were scattered throughout Judea and Samaria" (Acts 8:1). So how did all of the rank-and-file church members, most of whom were new in their faith, react to this life-threatening situation? Acts 8:4 tells us that "those who had been scattered *preached the word wherever they went*" (emphasis mine).

Wow! Talk about a contagious church—this community of believers was *unstoppable*! Evangelistic passion was the primary fuel it ran on. I believe that reaching lost people was the first among equals in terms of the early church's mission and values.

Likewise, if we want to become contagious churches, evangelism needs to become our top priority. Not our only priority—again, there needs to be a healthy, biblical balance—but the one that gets a higher portion of our attention, creativity, energy, and resources. As Bill Hybels discovered as a pastor and leader of a highly contagious church, we have to make what he called "a disproportionate investment in evangelism" if we're to have any hope of getting and keeping this value up to the level necessary.

Why must we make these extra efforts in this area? In part because, as we discussed earlier, this is the value that slips away the fastest—it's that pervasive age-old problem of *evangelistic entropy*. Also, I think, because of all the things we can focus on in our churches this is the one with the least "instant gratification." In other words, when you stretch yourself and make strides to reach lost people, nobody's likely to go out of their way to rush out and thank you! Later, when the impact is evident you might get some encouragement, but not at near the rate of return as for teaching a strong message to believers, leading a powerful worship service, or guiding a dynamic session with your small group. Invest your energies in evangelism and most non-Christians will ignore or resist you—and many believers will wonder why you're not giving more of your attention to them! The only immediate rewards are usually quiet and unseen, including silent whispers of affirmation from the Holy Spirit. Certainly wonderful—but not the kind of perk we can so easily get addicted to.

Finally, I think we need to make a greater investment in evangelism because this is the area that Satan fights against the hardest—since this is the one that feeds all the others. For example, do you want to have a teaching church? Evangelism provides a flow of people who desperately need to be taught. Want a worshiping church? Evangelism provides newly redeemed worshipers! A discipling church? Evangelism swells your ranks with fresh recruits who require discipling. How about a sending church? Evangelism can reach a pool of people out of which you can do the sending. Want to be a missionary church? Live out the evangelistic mission at home in ways that will prepare your people to take that mission other places. Want to be a Christ-honoring church? Help your people honor Christ by imitating his example and becoming friends of sinners who, like him, work "to seek and to save what was lost."

You see, if Satan's efforts, as well as church divisions, distractions, apathy, or obstacles stymie or shut down your evangelistic efforts, it will directly or indirectly affect every other goal and purpose of your church—so we must focus our greatest energy in this area and do so consistently over time.

## A BENCHMARK TO REACH FOR

But how much effort in evangelism is enough? How can we tell whether we're winning or losing in the outreach arena? These are difficult questions that warrant our attention.

As I've spoken with church leaders about the elements needed to become a highly evangelistic church, I've discovered a serious problem: what is considered "highly evangelistic" or "contagious" varies greatly from leader to leader and church to church. Some have huge, and perhaps unrealistic, expectations of what they should accomplish with respect to reaching lost people. This can lead to real frustration when they consistently fall short of their lofty goals.

But more often I find the opposite problem: leaders who have been long accustomed to seeing few to none coming to Christ through their outreach efforts can begin to think this situation is more or less normal. This can lead to their being too easily satisfied with only incrementally improved results. But we must not give up striving to attain our church's full evangelistic potential, which would result in our reaching even *one* less man, woman, or child than we could have otherwise reached.

Throughout these pages I've said very little about "church growth"—not because I'm against churches getting larger, but because it's so tempting to overemphasize numbers. When we focus too much on numeric growth, we can be tempted to start pursuing surface-level solutions and the recruitment of Christians from other churches, rather than doing the deep spadework of examining and strengthening our own hearts and habits for the sake of lost people who need God. So we've spent most of our energy on the 6-Stage Process designed to help us address these deeper issues, and then to lead, train, and mobilize our people in ways that can impact many for Christ.

But good news—when we do these things, it generally shows up on the numeric charts as well! The natural question is, what should these charts look like? How many people should a church reasonably expect to see coming to faith in a year? What would be a good benchmark to at least give us some idea of what we should shoot for?

I've thought long and hard about these questions. I've also prayed earnestly about whether to put a specific measure in this book—and, if so, which one. I only wanted to do so if it would be helpful, which meant it would need to be high enough to stretch us to do better, yet within reach so it would motivate us.

We've all heard grandiose scenarios like this one: If you reached one person today, and then you and that person each reached one more tomorrow, and then the four of you reached four more the next day, then eight more the next, and so on, a city the size of Chicago would be reached in twenty-four days, a country the size of the United States just five days later, and the entire world population—all seven or eight billion people—in a mere five more days, which is a total of only thirty-four days! The math really works. The problem is that this kind of "plan" fails to motivate anybody! It's hard enough to *reach the one person tomorrow*, let alone the increasingly unreasonable requirements on each successive day thereafter.

So it's tempting to discard these kinds of fantasy schemes and just throw up our hands and say, "Then let's not look at numbers at all. Let's just keep on doing the best we can, and let the results take care of themselves." But I think that would be a mistake. These "numbers" are not mere statistics—they're *changed lives!* They're human beings with names and faces, hopes and dreams, families and futures. They're people who matter to God. They're your husband or wife, father or mother, son or daughter, niece or nephew, neighbor or coworker—individuals you love and want to have with you in heaven for all of eternity. And if you have four or five of these people in your life—people your heart aches to reach—then you don't mind keeping track of which of them have come to faith. We're simply talking about doing this on a churchwide level.

By the way, do you know what they did in the New Testament? *They kept track!* Look at a few excerpts from the book of Acts (emphases mine):

- In those days Peter stood up among the believers (a group *numbering about a hundred and twenty*)—Acts 1:15.
- Those who accepted his message were baptized, and *about three thousand were added to their number that day*—Acts 2:41.
- And the Lord *added to their number daily* those who were being saved—Acts 2:47.
- But many who heard the message believed, and *the number of men grew to about five thousand*—Acts 4:4.
- Nevertheless, more and more men and women believed in the Lord and *were added to their number*—Acts 5:14.
- In those days ... *the number of disciples was increasing*—Acts 6:1.
- So the word of God spread. The *number of disciples in Jerusalem increased rapidly*, and *a large number of priests* became obedient to the faith—Acts 6:7.
- Then the church throughout Judea, Galilee and Samaria enjoyed a time of peace. It was strengthened; and encouraged by the Holy Spirit, *it grew in numbers*, living in the fear of the Lord—Acts 9:31.

This list goes on, including nearly a dozen additional references just in the book of Acts alone. The leaders of the early church were not shy about looking at, talking about, or recording actual results—so neither should we.

As I prayed about a benchmark that would serve churches in fulfilling God's mission, I believe he led me to one that will be simultaneously challenging and realistic and simple enough to be easily understood and employed. (And what's interesting is that I "came up with this model" months before discovering that Dann Spader and Sonlife Ministries had been teaching and helping churches for a long time by means of this model,[1] and that Donald McGavran had proposed it years earlier!) Here's the measure:

> Every church, in cooperation with the work of the Holy Spirit, reaching and retaining one non-Christian per year for every ten Christians who are regular attenders. In other words, a church of 100 leading 10 people to Christ this year, adding them to their fold, and then next year that church of 110 reaching and enfolding 11 more, then the next year 121 reaching and enfolding 12, and so forth. Or, if you have a team of ten people who are planting a church together, reach at least one this year. When you get up to thirty, try to reach at least three. And some day if you grow to 1,500, pray and ask God to help you bring 150 non-Christians to Christ.

Remember, if you choose to adopt this it will be a *goal*, not a *limit*— God may bless your efforts way beyond this, at least for some seasons. Also, note that a church with these kinds of results will also naturally attract additional Christians who want to be "where the action is" (as discussed at the end of chapter three). That's fine, but don't count them as part of the 10 percent!

What I love about the model is that it's actually attainable; 100 people really can, by God's grace, reach 10. (One way to achieve this, theoretically, would be for each Frontline member—the 10 percent with gifts or passion for evangelism—to simply reach one person per year. But don't tell the congregation that—you want to get them all in on this adventure!) Yet it's also stretching—even for a megachurch of 10,000, which would be striving to reach 1,000 nonbelievers within a year's time.

The real challenge is to retain the people who are reached evangelistically and then build on this growth year after year (or redistribute it into newly planted congregations). But what's exciting is that, all else being equal, if you do this consistently, *your church will double in size every seven years*—by adding to your ranks freshly redeemed men, women, and children who will be motivated to help you reach even more!

What's more, if the evangelical churches in the United States would attain and sustain that level, we'd reach the entire nation in about thirty years—which is more or less within the life span of most of us reading this book. (And the situation would be similar in many other countries.) *Talk about a contagious epidemic!*

Now, let's put our feet back on the ground. Looking at a wide range of studies and statistics, the average rate—what church statisticians call "conversion growth rate"—for churches in America is between 2 and 3 percent (some are well above that level; many churches show no gain at all; and far too many are right now losing ground). This average is only about a fourth of what we're aiming for—the 10 percent rate—and, obviously, falls far short of fulfilling the Great Commission, where Jesus sweepingly tells us to "go into all the world and make disciples." So, needless to say, much work needs to be done.

The importance and benefits of this kind of benchmark were reinforced for me a while back when I spent some time with a group of evangelism leaders from some of the most outreach-oriented churches throughout the country. I shared this 10 percent evangelism growth model in order to get feedback and reactions from these ministry peers. While we had a lively discussion—a couple of them thought the rate was too low, and others weren't sure they wanted to count conversions at all—one man who had been active in most of the earlier discussions became uncharacteristically quiet.

Finally this committed evangelism leader spoke up in sober and vulnerable tones. He said, "You know, our church consists of 2,500 believers, and you're telling me we ought to be reaching 250 non-Christians this year. The truth is, we've only been trying to reach about 35. If we decided to try to reach 250, *we would have to change our whole way of thinking!*"

He was right! If we really want to achieve our churches' redemptive potential, most of us—and most of the other leaders and influencers in our churches—will have to change our whole way of thinking. In fact, *I think we're going to have to revolutionize the way we view and do evangelism.* We're going to have to declare war on every front, push back evangelistic entropy, and make reaching and retaining lost people our top priority. If we'll do this, I believe we can move toward, and in many cases even beyond, this 10 percent evangelistic growth rate.

My hope is that this model at least motivates you and your team to begin to measure, as best you can, how many people are really coming to faith each year through your church's collective efforts. If the number is just 1 percent of your congregation's present size, then start there. The important question for you would then be to figure out what it will take to get it up to 2 or 3 percent, and then to 5 percent and beyond. *Every* incremental gain is worth the effort and warrants celebrating, regardless of whether or not you ever hit the 10 percent goal!

## A NUMBERS GAME?

I spoke to a group of church leaders from various places at an all-day workshop, and I ended the day by presenting this 10 percent benchmark, and then saying, "Now, I don't want to turn this into a numbers game. If this model helps you, great; if not, just apply the 6-Stage Process and the other principles we've been talking about today, and let God handle the results."

I was about to close in prayer when Jim Ockenfels, a friend of mine who had been in the back of the room helping with the administrative aspects of the workshop, unexpectedly spoke up. "Mark, before you end I'd like to say something to everybody, if that's okay." Jim had come to faith just a few years earlier through the efforts and invitations of a contagious Christian coworker. Knowing his heart for lost people, as well as his passion to serve church leaders, I gladly agreed to let him say a few words. Still speaking from the back of the room, voice trembling and eyes filling with tears, Jim said with obvious conviction:

> *I'll* turn it into a "numbers game" for you: I'm the youngest of eleven children. There are seven of my brothers and sisters still living. None of them knows Christ. Out of the families of these seven, I've got twenty-one nieces and nephews, and fifty great-nieces and nephews. But of the seventy-eight people I just listed, only *three* know Christ as Savior.
>
> I've been praying all day for your churches, because they're spread out all over the country. I've been praying because I want there to be a contagious church out there for each of my relatives. That way, if they walk through your doors someday, they'll hear about Christ the way I did when I came to this church ...
>
> So that's my challenge for you: Build contagious churches and give these loved ones of mine the same kind of chance I had here!

Jim's powerful words helped us all that day to gain a deeper awareness of the immeasurable importance of the task at hand. I hope they serve you in the same way today.

## ELEMENTS FOR BECOMING A CONTAGIOUS CHURCH

In this closing section, I want to pull together the elements we've been talking about and add in a few other important ones, to help us get a handle on what we need to do in order to become truly contagious churches. These stand alongside the broader components of a biblically functioning church mentioned at the beginning of this chapter.

### Radical Commitment to Our Evangelistic Mission

Jesus, our ultimate Leader, said he came "to seek and to save what was lost" and to "give his life as a ransom for many." Jesus was laser focused on his evangelistic mission, and he was willing to give it all—and in fact *did* give it all—to fulfill that mission.

The apostle Paul said, "I consider my life worth nothing to me, if only I may finish the race and complete the task the Lord Jesus has given me—the task of testifying to the gospel of God's grace" (Acts 20:24). For Paul, too, there was no price too great to pay in the effort to reach people for Christ.

We've seen the sacrifice and the evangelistic dedication of the leaders in the New Testament church, recorded in the book of Acts. There are also the examples of the self-sacrificing church fathers, as well as countless early believers who laid down everything—often including their very lives—to serve and follow Christ and to strive to fulfill his redemptive purposes.

There was Martin Luther, who risked his life to nail the ninety-five theses to the door of Wittenberg's Castle Church and to translate the Scriptures into the language of the German people. And John Calvin, who sent missionaries into France and Brazil and pioneered the work of evangelism training at his Geneva Academy. And John Wesley, who rode all over the British Isles so he could bring the good news to the people there, and then sailed across the Atlantic so he could send preachers throughout the New World. There was William Booth, who fought against the status quo to start his mission of reaching people not just with words of love but also tangible expressions of loving service. And Dwight L. Moody, who gave of himself tirelessly to preach the gospel on both sides of the ocean, to print literature, to start schools, and to train young ministers. And Hudson Taylor, who risked and gave up everything to reach unchurched people in China, which was one of the most challenging mission fields in the world.

I believe that all these heroes of the faith, and countless other men and women who had big hearts and clear vision, understood what the church was about and saw what it could become—not just a cadre of committed believers, but a contagious community ready to attract, influence, and enfold nonbelievers all around them. They were leaders who gave of themselves to reach lost people with the life-changing message of the cross and then to disciple and grow them up into coworkers who would, in turn, give of themselves to reach still more. And I couldn't agree more with George Hunter when he says in his book *Church for the Unchurched*, "We do not honor our founders by blindly perpetuating in a changing world what they once did ... we honor them by doing for our time and culture what they did for theirs."[2]

It all starts in the hearts and lives of us as church leaders and influencers—ones who live evangelistic values (Stage 1), tirelessly work to instill those values in the people around us (Stage 2), and eagerly empower leaders who will join us in the task of becoming increasingly contagious churches (Stage 3).

## Willingness to Try Fresh Approaches

### In Existing Churches

Way back in the time of the prophet Jeremiah, God said he would "create a new thing on earth" (Jeremiah 31:22)—and it seems like God's people have been bent on keeping things the same ever since! We naturally gravitate toward the safety of sameness. But becoming a contagious church will require a new way of thinking, as well as the willingness and courage to put these ideas into action.

The great evangelist Billy Graham once wrote about what it will take "for the evangelistic imperative to be lived out in the future so that the twenty-first century becomes the greatest century for Christian evangelism in history." He said one of the things we need is:

> *A willingness to explore new methods and new fields.* Methods that have worked in the past to make people aware of the church and draw them into its programs will not necessarily work in a media-saturated age. It is no coincidence that those churches that are most often effective in reaching their neighborhoods and cities for Christ are often those that are the most flexible and adaptable in their methods.... The main point is that we need to stand back and be creative.[3]

It's not that we have to become antitradition; we just need to ask whether each tradition or practice is optimally serving the biblical purpose for which it was originally created. If it is, then keep it. If it's not, then within biblical guidelines find a better way.

Lee Strobel quotes the stinging words of the Southern Baptist missionary, Winston Crawley, who said, "If our efforts to share the gospel in today's world are limited only to the traditional model, then we have decided in advance on limited outreach and limited growth."

Let those words soak in for a moment or two. Are you willing to tie your own hands ahead of time so that, at most, you can expect only limited results? Neither am I. But that means, according to this Bible-based missionary, that we have to be ready, right now, to break out of the typical, traditional, status quo, "but-we've-always-done-it-this-way" models and expectations and start trying some exciting new things! It might feel a bit dangerous at first, but soon it'll be exhilarating as God's Spirit shows up, blesses your efforts, and starts leading more and more people to himself. When that happens, you and your team are going to wonder why you took so long to make some changes and get things moving!

### In New Churches

The need for flexibility and creativity does not apply merely to existing churches. Leaders who plant new churches must consider up front what they're trying to build and why. Beware of the temptation to simply duplicate old models and put a clone of the mother church in a new neighborhood for the mere reason that there isn't yet a franchise of this particular denominational "brand" in that area (whether there are other evangelical churches around the corner or not).

This can be a huge waste of kingdom resources! Now, don't get me wrong; I'm in favor of planting new churches. We just need to plant them *where they're really needed* and make sure we design them to fulfill the greatest need: *reaching and enfolding lost people.*

When you begin a new church, you've got an incredible opportunity to locate, focus, and build it in ways that will have a powerful evangelistic impact. And applying the 6-Stage Process—especially the first three stages—will help set the right evangelistic trajectory.

*Stage 1 for new churches:* If the leaders of the planting team will *live evangelistic lives* from the very beginning, they'll naturally implant these values into the DNA of the new church body. This will positively impact every decision and pattern of this church, both now and in the future. If, on the other hand, these values are set aside in the hopes of adding them later, after the church is "a bit more established," then old patterns will be set in spiritual cement, and it will be extremely difficult to alter the church's genetics and establish evangelism as a core value.

*Stage 2 for new churches:* If the church planting leadership works hard to *instill the value of evangelism* from the beginning, this will form a strong outreach culture and attract the right people who will partner to deepen and expand it. (It will also repel the wrong people while doing so is still fairly painless.) This value will create urgency, excitement, and a clear sense that this new work is part of a redemptive mission from God, and nothing else in the world could be more important!

*Stage 3 for new churches:* The church planting team should look and pray from the very beginning for *the right person to empower as its evangelism leader* who will protect and promote these values from the inception of the church. This will most likely be a key layperson, though it could someday become this person's full-time, adventure-filled career! I like what Rick Warren said about this in *The Purpose Driven® Church*:

> If I were starting a new church today I would begin by recruiting five volunteers for five unpaid staff positions ... [including someone to] oversee our evangelism and missions programs in the community. As the church grew I would move these people to part-time paid staff and eventually full-time.[4]

Following Stages 1–3 will help prepare the leaders and set the culture—both in new churches and in established ones—to then do the rest of what they need to in order to prepare and enroll the congregation to reach as many people as possible.

## Participation of the Entire Body

Effective, sustained evangelism is always a team activity. Jesus recruited twelve disciples and sent them out in pairs (Mark 6:7). Later he commissioned "seventy-two others and sent them two by two ahead of him" (Luke 10:1). After his death and resurrection, he gave the now-famous directive to his followers, "But you will receive power when the Holy Spirit comes on you; and you will be my witnesses in Jerusalem, and in all Judea and Samaria, and to the ends of the earth" (Acts 1:8). Within a matter of days, God miraculously used this team to speak to the crowds of people in their own languages (see Acts 2:6).

What impresses me about the powerful outreach and exponential growth of the early church is the broad participation of the entire group of ordinary Christ-followers: "After *they* prayed, the place where *they* were meeting was shaken. And *they were all filled* with the Holy Spirit *and spoke* the word of God boldly" (Acts 4:31, emphases mine). This was a contagious movement, and it involved *all* of the members of the church.

Every Christian is part of the church to which Jesus gave the Great Commission, and we each have a vital role to play. The task is too huge to be done on the backs of a few pastors, church leaders, or evangelism enthusiasts. We need nothing less than to *train every believer — 100 percent — to communicate Christ* and engage them in this evangelistic adventure in ways that are natural to them (Stage 4).

And we dare not neglect those to whom the Holy Spirit has given special gifts and passion to reach lost people with the gospel! This is a divine entrustment from God to the church, and we must carefully manage it as such. That's why, as we've discussed, many churches are beginning to catch the vision for starting *diverse, multistyled, and cross-departmental evangelism ministries* — like what I've called Frontline — to nurture, encourage, instruct, and empower their key outreach enthusiasts from around the church (Stage 5).

Once you've organized this diverse team of evangelism specialists, *watch out!* You've got the ingredients of a high-impact team of evangelists throughout the ministries of the church that can reach out on numerous fronts, from individualized outreach, to small group and classroom structures, to any level or shape of larger evangelistic event or ministry (Stage 6). And when you put gifted leadership behind that kind of evangelistic thrust, the results can be spiritually explosive!

Now that we've thoroughly explored the 6-Stage Process, let me point you and your team to the "6-Stage Process Assessment Tool" in the Appendix of this book (pages 209–218). It's a questionnaire you and your team can each fill out individually, following the directions there, and then compare your assessments with each other. Make sure you use this tool in a prayerful and constructive fashion. The goal is not to magnify or dwell on problems, but to look for positive ways to help your church become more evangelistically effective. May God lead and use this process!

## Maximization of Each Element of the Process

A final thought on the 6-Stage Process: On the one hand, the sequence of the stages is intentional and important. You can't spread a value you don't at least to some degree first own and live. You won't be able to empower an evangelism leader until at least a core of the church's influencers agree that the church needs to do more in this area. You won't be able to engage your congregation in evangelism training if the value is not first in some measure instilled in their hearts and in the church's culture. The Frontline concept of rallying all of the evangelism enthusiasts from all of the ministries depends upon the leadership and training elements. And the final stage of unleashing a variety of outreach ministries and events requires some degree of success in all of the earlier areas. So there's logic to the ordering of these stages and benefits to unfolding them in the prescribed order.

On the other hand, there's a danger in lingering too long on one stage in the perfectionistic hope of bringing it up to full speed before moving on to the next. This could take years—and it might never fully happen! For example, on a scale of 1 to 10, your pastor may be living the value of evangelism (Stage 1) at only about a 2 level. Chances are you'll never get him all the way up to a 10—and you might lose a couple of decades trying! Instead, do what you can to help him move up to a 3 or 4 (apply the relevant ideas from chapters two and three; also send him to great evangelism conferences, encourage him to visit evangelistically effective churches, give him and the other leaders copies of this book, etc.) and encourage him to cooperate with you and the other leaders in instilling this value in as many people in the congregation as possible (Stage 2). Maybe next you can only get Stage 2 to a 5 or 6 level, but that's enough to work within as you then find and empower an evangelism leader (Stage 3), and so forth. Advance as much as you can in each area, but keep moving through the process as quickly as you can.

Also, later stages can serve to strengthen earlier ones. For example, if you run a *Contagious Campaign* and train everyone in your church to share their faith (Stage 4), that will go a long way toward helping all of the leaders, along with the rest of the congregation, to really live this value (Stage 1) and to be motivated to spread and strengthen it throughout the church body (Stage 2). Again, the bottom line is this: Pay attention to the sequence of these elements, but advance each one as much you can, without getting stuck because an area won't move to the degree you hoped it would.

In addition, it's important to realize that your church may have natural strengths in one or more of these areas and that you don't need to hold back that area while you're trying to advance the others. For example, I know of a rapidly growing church that has always, from its inception, put on high-powered, outreach-effective weekend services (an expression of Stage 6) — ones that lead many people to Christ. But they have never trained their people in relational evangelism. Well, my counsel to that church's leaders was to keep doing what they do so well already, but at the same time to go back and reinforce the areas they're weak in, including training. Doing this will strengthen their impact, expand their outreach to people who won't visit their church or for whom there soon might not be enough seats, and make their already contagious church even more evangelistically effective.

## Alignment of the Church's Ministries and Services

It's highly possible, even probable, that while you're strengthening the evangelistic value throughout your church, various pockets of ministry will be unaffected and even resistant. These independent silos of activity will want to run unconstrained by the leadership and mission of the broader church. We can't afford to let this happen.

Many of these ministries and functions are fulfilling other important parts of the church's purposes, but as leaders we need to look at each area to make sure it's also being maximized, wherever appropriate, for the *outreach* side of the church's mission. We need to be certain that in each area we're applying the principle in Colossians 4:5: "Be wise in the way you act toward outsiders; make the most of every opportunity."

One way I've seen this accomplished is when the church's pastor and senior leaders meet a couple times a year with the directors of the various ministries to look at each ministry's goals and plans. They make certain that every ministry is staying focused and in sync with the overall direction of the church — including evangelism as a central purpose — or is clear on adjustments they need to make in order to do so. Plans are approved and resources allocated for the ones that are on track. In some situations, redirective leadership is applied to help a ministry better fulfill the mission for which it was originally created or, on rare occasions (if it has outlived its usefulness), to begin the process of bringing it to an end—which can be painful, but necessary. We can't afford to keep investing time, resources, and leadership into areas that are not fulfilling some aspect of our church's mission.

These meetings also give a natural forum for encouraging and affirming leaders and ministries, and provide a great place for synergistic interactions, troubleshooting, the sharing and cross-pollination of ideas, and prayer.

This process needs to be applied not only to individual ministries but also to the church as a whole. Throughout this book I've talked primarily about the activities of individual leaders and of ministries. But sooner or later, as the evangelistic mission and values take root, the larger structures and services of the church must also be examined. If you do this too early, it can cause unneeded stress and resistance. But eventually, as God leads, it becomes a natural part of applying the outreach values that are now shared and prevalent.

If we're really convinced that evangelism is central to the purpose of the entire church, we need to start looking at everything we do through an evangelistic lens—not so we can force everything to become unnaturally evangelistic, but so we can examine and be certain we're "making the most of every opportunity."

What about the main public services? Are they not only serving the needs of believers, but also conducted with "wisdom toward outsiders"? If not, what could be changed (without losing the main focus of worshiping God and building up believers)? Do we need to start a separate seeker-oriented service at a different time or evening? Can we get by with retuning our current worship service, making it more accessible to outsiders? Think carefully about the answer though; this option might ultimately be the right way for you, but far too many churches hide behind the idea of just being "a bit more attuned to spiritual seekers" and then change little or nothing. Many times they end up with the same old fare, with only superficial fixes and face-lifts that fail to address or relate to a truly unchurched visitor.

What about the music? What about the messages? What about the sound and the lights? What about the appearance of the building, the accessibility of the auditorium, and the times of the services? What about the attitude and appearance of the people who stand up front? What about the sign out by the road and the sayings or slogans on it? Does the name of the church open doors to people we hope to reach or close them?

What unnecessary barriers could be removed to make it easier for folks from the community to access our services, ministries, and ultimately, to understand and embrace our good news about Christ?

I'm fully aware I'm treading on sensitive territory! But becoming a contagious church will require you to do the same. The redemptive mission of the church is too important to let fear or traditional strongholds keep us from examining everything in light of our biblical, God-directed vision. We *must* align the entire church to accomplish its mission, including reaching lost people for Christ. We need to be wise about what to address when, but we must be courageous to move ahead as the Spirit leads.

## Strategic Coordination of Outreach Efforts

Throughout these pages we've talked about a number of strategic evangelistic activities and events, but there's a danger that we will think of each of them in isolation. When we do this, we fail to see the exponential gains that would have been possible with a more integrated approach, both with respect to planning and promotion.

For example, why not schedule Frontline meetings a week or two after the completion of a churchwide *Contagious Campaign* or a presentation of the *Becoming a Contagious Christian* seminar? To do so will allow you to explain and promote Frontline to fresh groups of people at the very point when they'll be the most motivated to attend.

Why not schedule evangelistic ministry meetings, such as seeker small group training or apologetics gatherings, as well as outreach events, to follow on the heels of Frontline meetings? This will allow you to cast vision and build excitement for these ministries at Frontline. This will also provide the opportunity to pray together about these initiatives with the people who will most naturally be motivated to do so.

At Christmas or Easter services, what well-placed printed or verbal invitations could be presented that would point holiday visitors to additional ministries and services of the church? What weekend sermon series could be announced? What special event for the children or students should be promoted?

If autumn is a season when a number of people decide to return to church, or if January is a time when well-meaning seekers make New Year's resolutions to help their families "get a little religious instruction," then how do you seize these moments to build momentum? If you're teaching a series on the questions skeptics ask, what could you do to encourage guests to visit a Q & A time or discussion group immediately after the service?

I can't answer these questions for you, but I can challenge you and your team to begin to think this way and to realize that *every* service, class, and event is an opportunity to point people toward additional next steps. Doing so will help them move forward in their spiritual journeys and deepen the evangelistic impact of your church.

## Sustaining Efforts in Spite of Resistance

Becoming a contagious church does not come naturally or easily, even for the most evangelistically committed leaders. There will be internal struggles and external resistance. The commitment will be costly in terms of time, finances, and sometimes pain-inducing change. Without question, the noble intention of prioritizing lost people will be challenged and sometimes even your motives will be questioned.

Jesus constantly faced these kinds of problems, as did Paul and Peter. As I read the Bible, it strikes me that after Peter obeyed the vision from heaven and courageously went into the house of Cornelius and led all who had gathered there to faith in Christ, he was almost immediately chastised by his fellow believers! Acts 11:1–2 says, "The apostles and the brothers throughout Judea heard that the Gentiles also had received the word of God. So when Peter went up to Jerusalem, the circumcised believers criticized him." This would be utterly shocking if it weren't such a familiar pattern in both the pages of Scripture and the experiences of risk-taking evangelistic leaders throughout history!

Within a few days of first noticing how the church members criticized Peter in that passage, I received an email message from a pastor friend in Australia who was leading his church toward greater evangelistic fruitfulness. He wrote:

> Why didn't you tell me that a church committed to reaching the unchurched was so hard to build? The only criticism so far is from Christians. Pretty sad.
>
> However, I'm pumped — it is so good to see people bringing their friends and then telling us how much their friends enjoyed it. It cannot get much better.
>
> Your mate, (his name)

I wrote him back and quoted from Luis Palau's booklet, *Heart for the World*:

> From the least to greatest, all true evangelists have been criticized, attacked, and even persecuted. That shouldn't surprise us, for "everyone who wants to live a godly life in Christ Jesus will be persecuted" (2 Timothy 3:12).... Most people who evangelize create waves. And when you create waves, a lot of people get upset.... Nevertheless it's a sign that you're doing something right when certain people begin to get upset because of what you represent and preach.[5]

It's often said that pioneers are the ones who get shot at the most. This is never fun, and most of us never get completely used to it. But we must remain faithful to the mission to which God has called us. Remember that our marching orders are from Jesus himself, and he is more than able to sustain us.

So stay the course. Overcome setbacks and acknowledge the mistakes you will inevitably make along the way. Review your biblical mission. Regroup your resources. Re-up your efforts. Along the way, tell lots of stories of the ways God is using these endeavors. Encourage members to share fresh testimonies. Celebrate even small successes. Let the congregation get a taste of the results that their prayers, courage, and hard work are producing.

## Unswerving Devotion to the Gospel

Beneath every evangelistic effort there must be a pure love for Christ and a wholehearted devotion to his gospel, which is "the power of God for the salvation of everyone who believes" (Romans 1:16). Incidentally, it's interesting to note that, as a general rule, the churches that are really growing around the world are those that have a high view of the Bible and place a strong emphasis on the need for every person to trust in Christ—demonstrating that God uses those who work with him, in his way, for his purposes.

## Commitment to Prayer and the Role of the Holy Spirit

We've talked a lot about evangelistic mission, values, and the 6-Stage Process. But let me remind us one more time of the real Power behind the process:

- No one seeks God unless he first seeks them (Romans 3:11).
- No one loves God except that he first loved them (1 John 4:19).
- No one comes to the Father except that he draws them (John 6:44).
- There would be no salvation but for the cross of Jesus Christ (Hebrews 9:22; 1 Peter 3:18) and the power of the gospel message (Romans 1:16).
- God is the ultimate evangelist, and we are simply servants in his redemptive enterprise (John 16:8–11).

Billy Graham puts it this way in the article I quoted earlier:

> Every success, every advance, no matter how slight, is possible only because God has been at work by the Holy Spirit. The Spirit gives us the message, leads us to those he has prepared, and brings conviction of sin and new life.... When we understand that truth, we also will realize the urgency of prayer in evangelism. My own ministry, I am convinced, has only been possible because of the countless men and women who have prayed.[6]

As I've shaped the thoughts that have gone into this book, I've struggled to determine where prayer best fits in this process. Should it be listed as Stage 1? Prayer always seems to precede effective evangelism. I quickly realized, however, that prayer cannot be relegated to one step in the process—it must permeate every part of it! So I've tried to weave it in *at every stage*. It intersects every step and gives it life. It is essential to the whole enterprise!

Korean church leader Billy Kim said, "Prayer is my first advice. Prayer is my second suggestion. And prayer is my third suggestion.... If I had to do it all over, I would do more praying and less preaching." Jim Cymbala, pastor of The Brooklyn Tabernacle, said in *Fresh Wind, Fresh Fire*, "If we are courageous enough to go on the spiritual attack, to be mighty men and women of prayer and faith, there is no limit to what God can accomplish through us.... What counts is bringing God's power and light into a dark world, seeing local communities touched by God as churches turn back from perilous apathy to become Holy Spirit centers of divine activity."[7]

## GOD IS STILL BUILDING HIS CHURCH

In the first chapter I told the story of "The Little Church That Could," Mount Carmel Community Church—the congregation that started with fifteen in a town with an entire population of 130! God has done exciting things through that once-tiny congregation.

Many stories could be told of churches of many different sizes, styles, and settings that have focused on their evangelistic mission and experienced, through God's power, dramatic results. Let me share just one exciting email:

> The baptism was incredible! 158 participants and packed services. The mom of one of our leaders came to watch her niece be baptized and then accepted Christ herself at the first service. She then reconciled with her two daughters and asked to be baptized at the next service by her daughter with whom she had just reconciled! There are many more stories like this. We were all in *awe*! Praise God!

I hope your heart rejoices as mine does over reports like this from other churches. But ultimately this book is not about other churches; it's about *your* church and what you and your team will do in cooperation with God's Spirit to make it a more contagious place. Jesus declared, "I will build my church" (Matthew 16:18), and he explained that, "This is to my Father's glory, that you bear much fruit" (John 15:8).

So, in light of what *God wants to do*, I can tell you with confidence that *he's willing to guide, bless, and use you to reach others!* Act now; start with the heart, take the necessary steps, lean on God at all times, and watch him work through you and your church!

A daunting task? Yes, in some ways—but let me remind you of some of the resources backing you up. You have:

- *The Father*—who "so loved the world that he gave his one and only Son."
- *Jesus Christ*—who came "to seek and to save what was lost" and to "give his life as a ransom for many."
- *The Holy Spirit*—who is right now convicting the world of sin, drawing people to Christ, and empowering your efforts.
- *The gospel*—which is "the power of God for the salvation of everyone who believes."
- *Prayer*—along with the assurance that God "is able to do immeasurably more than all we ask or imagine."
- *Spiritual gifts*—with which God equips every member of his church for a strategic role in this great redemptive drama.

- *The Word of God*—which is "sharper than any double-edged sword" and which will not return to him empty.
- *The promises of God*—which assure us of his protection, power, and provision.
- *The Great Commission*—which reminds us that evangelism is God's idea, and promises Christ's presence with us to the very end of the age.

God's divine power truly has given us "everything we need for life and godliness" (2 Peter 1:3)—and, I think I'm safe to add, for *ministry* as well! So, I ask you, in the inspired words of the apostle Paul, "If God is for us, who can be against us?" (Romans 8:31).

God *is* for us. And as we seek to become contagious churches that expand the borders of his kingdom, he'll be *with* us too, helping us complete the work and produce good fruit in the form of countless lives impacted for all eternity.

## TO CONSIDER AND DISCUSS

1. Looking at the broader picture of a contagious church, are there areas *other than evangelism* where you think your church could use some shoring up in order to better attract and retain outsiders?

2. What could you do personally to help make the things you listed happen?

3. Reflect on the evangelistic growth rate for your church. Estimate how many people trusted in Christ through the ministry of your church in the last year and who now attend, and divide it by the number of weekly attenders (for example, nine new believers, divided by 150 attenders, would come out as .06, or a 6 percent rate).

   _____ (came to faith and attend the church), divided by _____ (average attendance) = _____ percent

   If you'd like to see that number move up, what increase will you pray and work toward, and by what date would you hope to reach it?

   Desired rate: _____ percent    by date: _____

4. Skim through the headings in this chapter under the section labeled "Elements for Becoming a Contagious Church." Identify the areas where you think a concentrated effort is most needed in your church. List them in order of priority.

#1 _____

_____

#2 _____

_____

#3 _____

_____

5. How can you best help your church make progress in these areas?

6. Take time to pray right now, alone or with a group, for your church's efforts to reach increasing numbers of people for Christ.

# ACKNOWLEDGMENTS

## FOR THE ORIGINAL *BUILDING A CONTAGIOUS CHURCH* BOOK, 2000

This book would have never been written without the strength and grace of God, as well as the love, support, encouragement, and prayers of many faithful friends and family members. I am indebted to numerous people, including:

My wife, Heidi, for your unwavering support from the day we wrote down the initial outline to the recent morning when you helped me organize the final edits—you've cheered me on all along the way like nobody else could. Matthew, for your faith-filled prayers each night, and Emma Jean, for your sweet words of encouragement each day. In addition, thanks to all three of you for your enduring patience and the inspiring posters and notes to cheer me along the way.

Lee Strobel, for your ideas, advice, and input—and faithful friendship that never changes, whether we live near or far! Bill Hybels, for your support, the ministry opportunities you've opened for me, your modeling of a contagious Christian life, as well as the several messages used in this book. Don Cousins, for strong influence early in my ministry that has shaped my thinking and approach in many important ways.

Karl and Barbara Singer, for extraordinary help and a home away from home where I could get so much writing done. Kevin and Sherry Harney, for researching and collecting stories from contagious churches all over the country, your fervent prayers, and the inspiring email and voice mail messages. Rickey Bolden, for encouraging me to take the first steps and for spurring me on throughout the process. Laura Dorans, for your undying support and assistance. Brad Mitchell, for constantly unleashing your encouragement gift on me.

Jack Kuhatschek at Zondervan, for genuinely caring, understanding, and helping to shape the book, as well as Dirk Buursma, for passionate commitment to making every word and detail right, and Stan Gundry, for believing in and supporting this project from the beginning.

Jim Mellado and the leadership team of the Willow Creek Association, for your enthusiasm about this ministry resource and your support during the many steps of its development. The team also includes Gary Schwammlein, Sharon Swing, Steve Bell, Tripp Stegall, and Joe Sherman (who initially helped prompt me to develop this tool), as well as former leadership team members, John Williams and Wende Lindsey-Kotouc. You've all been a great encouragement.

The friends and ministry colleagues who prayed and gave a wealth of support in a variety of ways and at various stages, including Garry Poole, Russ and Lynn Robinson, Paul Braoudakis, Bob Gordon, Judson Poling, Wendy Seidman, Cathy Burnett, Christine Anderson, Doug Yonamine, Tammy Burke, David Hannah, Tom and Robin Smith, Mindy Thompson, Lynn Norum, Larry and Rosemary Estry (especially the distant middle-of-the-night prayers!), Marie Little, Renee McMurry, Kari Lesser, Ashley Podgorski, Jeff Johnson, Rob and Tone Gorman, Mark Edwards, Bill Conard, Mark Miller, Steve Pate, Gary and Sheri Kingsbury, Jen Barr, Kimberly Knoll, Larry O'Reilly, Bob and Julie Harney, Tom and Nancy Vitacco, Chad Meister, Tom Youngblood, Stan Kellner, Bryan Hochhalter, Wanda Fogarty, Nancy Grisham, Lon Allison, Rick Richardson, Brad Smith, Dann Spader, Marc Harrienger, Dave and Sandy Gelwicks, Ron Seyk, Lance Murdock, and Rich and Mary Verlare.

Finally and especially, thanks to my wonderful family members who prayed for this project and encouraged me throughout, including my parents, Orland and Ginny Mittelberg; my grandmother, Effa Mittelberg; my sisters, Kathy and Lisa; my brother, Gary; and my father- and mother-in-law, Hillis and Jean Hugelen.

## FOR THE UPDATED *BECOMING A CONTAGIOUS CHURCH* BOOK, 2007

In addition to the acknowledgments above, I'd like to thank John Raymond and Mike Cook at Zondervan for your vision and support for this new, updated edition (with the slightly revised title), *Becoming a Contagious Church*. I'd also like to thank, as always, my ministry partner, Lee Strobel, for all of your ideas, encouragement, and help along the way, as well as my good friends Nancy Grisham and Brad Mitchell for your help in reading and providing feedback on the updated manuscript. May God be honored by all of our efforts and use this book to encourage and inspire churches around the world to reach many more people for Christ.

# 6-STAGE PROCESS ASSESSMENT TOOL

Instructions: Even if you're discussing this with a group, *individually* rate each statement on pages 209–215 using the following scale:

> 5 = Strongly Agree
> 4 = Agree
> 3 = Partially Agree
> 2 = Disagree
> 1 = Strongly Disagree

Total your numbers for each stage as you go. Scoring instructions for the assessment are found on page 216.

## STAGE 1: LIVE AN EVANGELISTIC LIFE

### Personal

*Rating*

I am passionate about leading others to Christ.

People could accurately label me a "friend of sinners."

I am ready to share the gospel whenever there is an opportunity.

I frequently pray for specific lost people by name.

I have weekly contact with non-Christians who I am trying to win to Christ.

I intentionally take risks to start spiritual conversations with nonbelieving friends.

### Church Leadership

The majority of our church's leaders (pastor/s, key leaders, deacons, elders, etc.):

—are passionate about reaching lost people for Christ. _____

—could individually be labeled as a "friend of sinners." _____

—are ready to share the gospel whenever there is an opportunity. _____

—pray for specific lost people by name. _____

—make it a high priority to spend time with non-Christians whom they are trying to win to Christ. _____

—regularly take risks to start spiritual conversations with their lost friends. _____

*Total for Stage 1* _____

## STAGE 2: INSTILL EVANGELISTIC VALUES IN THE PEOPLE AROUND YOU

*Rating*

I pray regularly for others in my church to become passionate about reaching their lost friends and family for Christ. _____

Reaching lost people is a nonnegotiable priority that our church lives out on a consistent basis. _____

I frequently encourage and motivate others with my evangelism stories. _____

At our church, it's normal for us to pray for evangelistic effectiveness. _____

Our congregation is regularly taught (from the pulpit, small groups, Sunday school, etc.) how to establish and deepen relationships with nonbelievers. _____

It is clear to our people that evangelism is central to the mission of our church. _____

From the pulpit, our church has "declared war" in our efforts to raise the value of evangelism.     _____

Using personal stories, key Scripture passages, or testimonies our pastor regularly preaches messages that raise the value that lost people matter to God and should matter to us.     _____

People in our church understand that God has equipped believers differently regarding their approach to evangelism.     _____

Our church budget reflects the priority of evangelism in our church.     _____

Our church celebrates ordinary Christians who participate in outreach.     _____

Our church is known in the community for prioritizing and reaching out to people who are far from God.     _____

*Total for Stage 2*     _____

## STAGE 3: EMPOWER AN EVANGELISM LEADER

*Rating*

Our senior pastor recognizes that he/she cannot personally lead the evangelism ministry as well as oversee the overall ministry direction of the church.     _____

In our church, someone other than the senior pastor has been officially empowered to be the evangelism leader.     _____

Our church leaders hold the evangelism leader primarily accountable for results in the area of evangelism and encourage and pray for him/her.     _____

Our evangelism leader:

—is passionate about partnering with others to reach their friends for Christ.     _____

—effectively influences and leads other ministries in our church to keep the evangelism value high. _____

—has proven leadership skills, and relates well to a broad spectrum of people. _____

—has a strong desire to train and equip others to communicate their faith. _____

—has no other major ministry responsibilities besides evangelism. _____

—is able to effectively articulate and defend Christian doctrine. _____

—encourages and equips our congregation to use their own individual evangelism styles when reaching their friends. _____

—is empowered by our church leadership to do what needs to be done in the area of evangelism. _____

—has been provided adequate resources to fund our church's evangelism efforts. _____

*Total for Stage 3* _____

## STAGE 4: TRAIN THE CHURCH IN EVANGELISM SKILLS—THE 100 PERCENT

*Rating*

In our church, every believer understands that he or she has a significant role and responsibility in evangelism. _____

Our church has begun to execute a plan to equip every believer to communicate his or her faith effectively. _____

All of our paid staff have been through evangelism training within the last two to three years. _____

All of our lay leaders have been through evangelism training within the last two to three years. _____

We offer evangelism training multiple times and in a variety of settings every year. _____

Every believer is challenged to discover and use his or her own style of evangelism. _____

Our people are trained and able to raise spiritual topics in a natural way during ordinary conversations. _____

Our people are equipped to share their personal story/ testimony with those outside the faith. _____

All of the believers in our church family can effectively communicate the gospel message. _____

Our attenders are able to pray with someone and lead them across the line of faith. _____

A majority of our church family is in the process of building relationships with lost people with the intention of sharing Christ with them. _____

For the most part, the believers in our church feel fairly comfortable answering spiritual questions raised by their seeking friends. _____

*Total for Stage 4* _____

## STAGE 5: MOBILIZE THE CHURCH'S EVANGELISM SPECIALISTS—THE 10 PERCENT

*Rating*

Our church has established an evangelism ministry to inspire and inform those who have evangelistic passion and/or gifts. _____

Most of the individuals who participate in our evangelism meetings are encouraged to stay in their current ministry to raise and reinforce the value of evangelism there. _____

Our evangelism ministry meets three to six times a year. _____

Fresh evangelism stories are shared as part of every evangelism meeting. _____

Teaching and skills reinforcement are a consistent part of evangelism ministry meetings. _____

During our meetings, we highlight and explain upcoming evangelistic training opportunities and outreach events. _____

Significant effort has been invested to identify the evangelistic core of our church. _____

Evangelism ministry meetings are used as a forum to introduce proven outreach tools and resources. _____

Evangelism ministry meetings are used as an opportunity to thank and celebrate people for their role in evangelism. _____

Prayer is always a component of our evangelism ministry meetings. _____

Our evangelism ministry includes, supports, and celebrates believers with a wide variety of evangelistic styles. _____

Our evangelism ministry is seen as a partner—not a competitor—to the other ministries in our church. _____

*Total for Stage 5* _____

## STAGE 6: UNLEASH AN ARRAY OF OUTREACH MINISTRIES AND EVENTS

*Rating*

Our church is excited about the synergy of utilizing both individual evangelism efforts and church-sponsored outreach events. _____

Our church hosts multiple outreach events each year designed specifically for believers to bring their lost friends. _____

The majority of our congregation actually brings unchurched people to our outreach ministries and events. _____

Our believers view our outreach events as a catalyst for starting spiritual conversations and use them that way. _____

All of our outreach ministries and events have clearly stated objectives. _____

It's generally clear what group or groups of people each outreach ministry and event is designed for. _____

Leading up to special churchwide outreach events, the teaching from the pulpit challenges and prepares our people to invite their unchurched friends. _____

Our guests at these events often comment on the relevance of the topic or presentation to their lives. _____

We consistently get positive feedback from our members regarding the level of excellence we exhibit in our various outreach ministries and events. _____

Every outreach event provides visitors with next steps they can take for further growth and involvement in the church. _____

Prayer permeates the entire process of creating and executing our outreach events. _____

Every outreach ministry and event is evaluated to determine its effectiveness and to improve upon it the next time. _____

*Total for Stage 6* _____

## PROCESSING YOUR RESULTS AND NEXT STEPS

1. After you complete the individual assessment, total your numbers in each section. Post your six totals to the summary list below, under "My Total."

   Please note that each stage has a 12–60 point scale, which might be interpreted as follows:

   | | |
   |---|---|
   | A rating of 12–28 | means you're at the beginning level with that stage. |
   | A rating of 29–44 | means you have some level of activity with that stage, but work still needs to be done. |
   | A rating of 45–60 | means you're well on your way! |

2. Working with your ministry team to calculate a team average, ask each individual to share his or her total for each stage. Add up their numbers and divide the total for each stage by the number of people in your group. Post the results under "Team Average." This will give you a preliminary snapshot of your team's assessment of where your church stands right now on each stage of the 6-Stage Process.

### Score Summary:

| | My Total | Team Average |
|---|---|---|
| Stage 1: LIVE an Evangelistic Life | _____ | _____ |
| Stage 2: INSTILL Evangelistic Values in the People around You | _____ | _____ |
| Stage 3: EMPOWER an Evangelism Leader | _____ | _____ |
| Stage 4: TRAIN the Church in Evangelism Skills—the 100 Percent | _____ | _____ |

Stage 5: MOBILIZE the Church's
Evangelism Specialists — the
10 Percent                    _____    _____

Stage 6: UNLEASH an Array of
Outreach Ministries and
Events                        _____    _____

3. Now discuss with your group the specific characteristics of each stage, focusing your time right now primarily on Stages 1 and 2. Your objective is to understand everyone's point of view and learn all you can from the group members. Differences of opinion are to be expected. Resist the temptation to find the "correct" answer or to put anyone on the spot. Listen carefully to try to understand why someone rated an item as he or she did. The primary value of this assessment is to begin constructive dialogue and provide clues regarding potential next steps.

4. After everyone has shared his or her individual responses and you have a sense of where you think you and your church stand overall, begin a discussion of priorities. What positive and practical steps can you and your group take (or encourage others in your church to take) to shore up any weak areas — especially in Stages 1 and 2, which are so foundational?

5. In trying to establish priorities, talk as a group through the following questions:

- What has this *discussion* told us about where we need to focus our efforts to improve and grow?
- How do the *numbers* further inform us? What do they tell us about each stage? In particular, what do they tell us about Stages 1 and 2?
- What has the *Holy Spirit* been saying to our group—or to anyone in our group—about what our next steps need to be?

NOTE: Please remember that this book, *Becoming a Contagious Church*, is designed to be a resource to your team and your entire church, giving you lots of ideas for next steps within each of the six stages. Specifically, chapters two through seven cover each of the stages, one per chapter. You may want to have your group members read a chapter each week and then meet to discuss each one together.

6. When thinking about specific ideas regarding what to do next, answer the following question: *Who will do what, by when?* Write down these plans today, even if preliminarily, and follow up the next time your group meets.

| What will we do? | Whose primary responsibility is it? | By when? |
|---|---|---|
| _____ | _____ | _____ |
| _____ | _____ | _____ |
| _____ | _____ | _____ |
| _____ | _____ | _____ |
| _____ | _____ | _____ |

7. Before you end your discussion, we encourage you to pray for yourself, for each other, for your church, and for the next steps you've written down—knowing that God wants to use and bless you in your efforts to build his kingdom.

# NOTES

## CHAPTER 1: YOUR CHURCH REACHING LOST PEOPLE

1. Cited by George Barna in his seminar and handbook "What Effective Churches Have Discovered," 1996. Some recent studies, however, indicate an encouraging upward trend in churches providing evangelism training.
2. Bill Hybels and Mark Mittelberg, *Becoming a Contagious Christian* (Grand Rapids: Zondervan, 1994); Mark Mittelberg, Lee Strobel, and Bill Hybels, the revised and updated *Becoming a Contagious Christian* evangelism course and campaign (Grand Rapids, Mich: Zondervan, 2007).
3. Henry Blackaby and Claude King, *Experiencing God: Knowing and Doing the Will of God* (Nashville: LifeWay Christian Resources, 1990).

## CHAPTER 2: STAGE 1: LIVE AN EVANGELISTIC LIFE

1. Sam Walton, *Sam Walton, Made in America: My Story* (New York: Doubleday, 1992), 188.
2. Robert Coleman, *The Master Plan of Evangelism*, 2nd ed. (Grand Rapids, Mich.: Revell, 1993).
3. Rebecca Manley Pippert, *Out of the Saltshaker and Into the World* (Downers Grove, Ill.: InterVarsity Press, 1979, updated 1999).
4. Joe Aldrich, *Lifestyle Evangelism* (Portland, Ore.: Multnomah, 1999).
5. Lyle Dorsett, *A Passion for Souls* (Chicago: Moody Press, 1997).
6. Billy Graham, *Just As I Am: An Autobiography of Billy Graham* (San Francisco: HarperSanFrancisco, 1997).
7. Rick Warren, *The Purpose Driven Church* (Grand Rapids, Mich.: Zondervan, 1995).
8. Michael Richardson, *Amazing Faith: The Authorized Biography of Bill Bright* (Colorado Springs: WaterBrook, 2001).

## CHAPTER 3: STAGE 2: INSTILL EVANGELISTIC VALUES IN THE PEOPLE AROUND YOU

1. Rick Warren, *The Purpose Driven Church* (Grand Rapids, Mich.: Zondervan, 1995), 82.
2. Sam Walton, *Sam Walton, Made in America: My Story* (New York: Doubleday, 1992), 173.
3. Walton, *Sam Walton, Made in America*, 221.
4. Walton, *Sam Walton, Made in America*, 223.

5. Wayne Cordeiro, *Doing Church as a Team* (Honolulu: New Hope Christian Fellowship O'ahu, 1998), 163–64.

6. John Kotter, *Leading Change* (Boston: Harvard Business School Press, 1996), 36.

7. The six sermon transcripts in the *Contagious Campaign* are included on the CD-ROM in the revised and updated *Becoming a Contagious Christian* training course curriculum kit (Grand Rapids, Mich.: Zondervan, 2007).

8. Bill Hybels, *Just Walk Across the Room* (Grand Rapids, Mich.: Zondervan, 2006).

9. Mark Mittelberg, Lee Strobel, and Bill Hybels, *Becoming a Contagious Christian Leader's Guide*, rev. and updated ed. (Grand Rapids, Mich.: Zondervan, 2007), 116–118.

10. Everett Rogers, *The Diffusion of Innovations*, 4th ed. (New York: Free Press, 1995).

11. The National Outreach Convention is sponsored annually by Outreach, Inc.: www.outreach.com, phone 800-991-6011.

12. George Barna, *Evangelism That Works* (Ventura, Calif.: Gospel Light, 1995), 84.

13. For more information on this process, I recommend the book *How to Change Your Church (Without Killing It)*, by Alan Nelson and Gene Appel (Nashville: Word, 2000).

14. Barna, *Evangelism That Works*, 100.

## CHAPTER 4: STAGE 3: EMPOWER AN EVANGELISM LEADER

1. Bruce Bugbee, *What You Do Best in the Body of Christ*, rev. ed. (Grand Rapids, Mich.: Zondervan, 2005).

2. Greg Ogden, *Unfinished Business: Returning the Ministry to the People of God* (Grand Rapids, Mich.: Zondervan, 1990).

3. Bruce Bugbee and Don Cousins, *Network: The Right People, in the Right Places, for the Right Reasons, at the Right Time*, rev. ed. (Grand Rapids, Mich.: Zondervan, 2005).

4. Robert S. McNamara, *In Retrospect: The Tragedy and Lessons of Vietnam* (New York: Time Books, 1995), 332.

5. George Barna, *Evangelism That Works* (Ventura, Calif.: Gospel Light, 1995), 97. Emphasis added.

6. Barna, *Evangelism That Works*, 97.

7. Barna, *Evangelism That Works*, 136–37.

## CHAPTER 5: STAGE 4: TRAIN THE CHURCH IN EVANGELISM SKILLS—THE 100 PERCENT

1. For further information on the evangelism styles, see session two of the *Becoming a Contagious Christian* training course and chapter nine of the *Becoming a Contagious Christian* book.

2. Mark Mittelberg, Lee Strobel, and Bill Hybels, *Becoming a Contagious Christian Youth Edition*, rev. and expanded for students by Bo Boshers (Grand Rapids, Mich.: Zondervan, 2000).

## CHAPTER 6: STAGE 5: MOBILIZE THE CHURCH'S EVANGELISM SPECIALISTS — THE 10 PERCENT

1. George Barna, *Evangelism That Works* (Ventura, Calif.: Gospel Light, 1995), 100, emphasis added.
2. *Outreach* magazine is published by Outreach, Inc., www.outreachmagazine.com, phone 800-991-6011 or 760-940-0600.
3. *The Journey: A Bible for the Spiritually Curious* (Grand Rapids, Mich.: Zondervan; South Barrington, Ill.: Willow Creek Association, 1996).
4. Lee Strobel, *The Case for Christ* (Grand Rapids, Mich.: Zondervan, 1998); *The Case for Faith* (Grand Rapids, Mich.: Zondervan, 2000); *The Case for a Creator* (Grand Rapids, Mich.: Zondervan, 2004); *The Case for the Real Jesus* (Grand Rapids, Mich.: Zondervan, 2007).
5. Josh McDowell, *More Than a Carpenter* (Wheaton, Ill.: Tyndale, 1977).
6. Robert Laidlaw, *The Reason Why* (Grand Rapids, Mich.: Zondervan, 1970).
7. Garry Poole and Judson Poling, *Tough Questions*, rev. ed., series of seven study guides for seeker small groups (Grand Rapids, Mich.: Zondervan, 2003).

## CHAPTER 7: STAGE 6: UNLEASH AN ARRAY OF OUTREACH MINISTRIES AND EVENTS

1. George Barna, *Marketing the Church* (Colorado Springs: NavPress, 1988), 111.
2. Garry Poole, *Seeker Small Groups* (Grand Rapids, Mich.: Zondervan, 2003).
3. Garry Poole and Judson Poling, *Tough Questions*, rev. ed., series of seven study guides for seeker small groups (Grand Rapids, Mich.: Zondervan, 2003).
4. Rick Warren, *The Purpose Driven Church* (Grand Rapids, Mich.: Zondervan, 1995), 157–58.
5. Stan Telchin, *Betrayed!* (Grand Rapids, Mich.: Chosen Books, 1982).
6. Phillip E. Johnson, *Darwin on Trial* (Downers Grove, Ill.: InterVarsity Press, 1993).
7. Philip Doddridge, "O Happy Day!" *Praise! Our Songs and Hymns* (Grand Rapids, Mich.: Singspiration Music, 1979), 275.
8. Lee Strobel, *Inside the Mind of Unchurched Harry and Mary* (Grand Rapids, Mich.: Zondervan, 1993), 159.
9. *Atheism Versus Christianity* VHS videotape (Grand Rapids, Mich.: Zondervan, 1994).
10. For information on the evangelism styles, see chapter five in this book, session two of the *Becoming a Contagious Christian* training course, and chapter nine of the *Becoming a Contagious Christian* book.

11. Kevin Harney is the author of *Seismic Shifts* (Zondervan, 2005), a book that discusses in part some of these evangelism ideas.

## CHAPTER 8: COMMUNICATING THE GOSPEL WITHOUT COMPROMISE

1. Bill Hybels and Mark Mittelberg, *Becoming a Contagious Christian* (Grand Rapids, Mich.: Zondervan, 1994), 209.
2. Lee Strobel, *The Case for Christ* (Grand Rapids, Mich.: Zondervan, 1998); Lee Strobel, *The Case for Faith* (Grand Rapids, Mich.: Zondervan, 2000); Lee Strobel, *The Case for the Real Jesus* (Grand Rapids, Mich.: Zondervan, 2007).
3. Josh McDowell, *More Than a Carpenter* (Wheaton, Ill.: Tyndale, 1977).
4. Paul Little, *Know Why You Believe*, 2nd ed. (Downers Grove, Ill.: InterVarsity Press, 2000).
5. Norman L. Geisler and William E. Nix, *A General Introduction to the Bible*, rev. ed. (Chicago: Moody Press, 1986).
6. Bill Hybels, "The Core Idea," Seeds tape series (available through the Willow Creek Association at 800-570-9812).
7. George Barna, *The Barna Report*, bimonthly newsletter, October 1999, 4.
8. *The Journey: A Bible for the Spiritually Curious* (Grand Rapids, Mich.: Zondervan, South Barrington, Ill.: Willow Creek Association, 1996).

## CHAPTER 9: CONTAGIOUS CHURCHES AND THE UNSTOPPABLE SPREAD OF THE CHRISTIAN FAITH

1. For information on Sonlife, call 800-770-4769 or 630-762-9900, or visit www.sonlife.com.
2. George Hunter, *Church for the Unchurched* (Nashville: Abingdon, 1996), 67.
3. Billy Graham, "Recovering the Primacy of Evangelism," *Christianity Today*, 8 December 1997, 29–30.
4. Rick Warren, *The Purpose Driven Church* (Grand Rapids, Mich.: Zondervan, 1995), 147.
5. Luis Palau, "Heart for the World" (Portland, Ore.: Luis Palau Evangelistic Association, 1989), 9–10.
6. Graham, "Recovering the Primacy of Evangelism," 30.
7. Jim Cymbala, *Fresh Wind, Fresh Fire* (Grand Rapids, Mich.: Zondervan, 1997), 181–82.

**WILLOW**
Willow Creek Association

# Willow Creek Association
*Vision, Training, Resources for Prevailing Churches*

This resource was created to serve you and to help you build a local church that prevails. It is just one of many ministry tools that are part of the Willow Creek Resources® line, published by the Willow Creek Association together with Zondervan.

The Willow Creek Association (WCA) was created in 1992 to serve a rapidly growing number of churches from across the denominational spectrum that are committed to helping unchurched people become fully devoted followers of Christ. Membership in the WCA now numbers over 12,000 Member Churches worldwide from more than ninety denominations.

The Willow Creek Association links like-minded Christian leaders with each other and with strategic vision, training, and resources in order to help them build prevailing churches designed to reach their redemptive potential. Here are some of the ways the WCA does that.

- **The Leadership Summit**—a once a year, two-and-a-half-day conference to envision and equip Christians with leadership gifts and responsibilities. Presented live at Willow Creek as well as via satellite broadcast to over 130 locations across North America, this event is designed to increase the leadership effectiveness of pastors, ministry staff, volunteer church leaders, and Christians in the marketplace.

- **Ministry-Specific Conferences**—throughout each year the WCA hosts a variety of conferences and training events—both at Willow Creek's main campus and offsite, across the U.S., and around the world—targeting church leaders and volunteers in ministry-specific areas such as: small groups, preaching and teaching, the arts, children, students, volunteers, stewardship, etc.

- **Willow Creek Resources®**—provides churches with trusted and field-tested ministry resources in such areas as leadership, evangelism, spiritual formation, spiritual gifts, small groups, stewardship, student ministry, children's ministry, the use of the arts-drama, media, contemporary music—and more.

- **WCA Member Benefits**—includes substantial discounts to WCA training events, a 20 percent discount on all Willow Creek Resources®, *Defining Moments* monthly audio journal for leaders, quarterly *Willow* magazine, access to a Members-Only section on WillowNet, monthly communications, and more. Member Churches also receive special discounts and premier services through WCA's growing number of ministry partners—Select Service Providers—and save an average of $500 annually depending on the level of engagement.

For specific information about WCA conferences, resources, membership, and other ministry services contact:

**Willow Creek Association**
P.O. Box 3188, Barrington, IL 60011-3188
Phone: 847-570-9812, Fax: 847-765-5046

www.willowcreek.com

# Becoming a Contagious Christian Curriculum

## Communicating Your Faith in a Style That Fits You

*Mark Mittelberg, Lee Strobel, and Bill Hybels*

Releasing the hidden evangelist in every Christian — Picture all of your church members as evangelists who: Demonstrate a contagious Christian character . . . Build spiritually strategic relationships . . . Direct conversations toward matters of faith . . . Communicate their faith in a style that's personal and natural . . . Explain biblical truths in a style that's personal and natural . . . Explain biblical truths in everyday language . . . Respond to the most common objections to Christianity.

*Becoming a Contagious Christian* is a proven course designed to equip believers for effective evangelism in today's world. It avoids stereotyped approaches that feel intimidating to many Christians. Instead, it shows ordinary believers how they can share the gospel in a natural and powerful way while being the person God made them to be. Each session's exercises, discussions, self-assessments, and video vignettes give step-by-step guidance to help participants become effective communicators for Christ to those around them. Used with nearly 1,000,000 people — *Becoming a Contagious Christian* is an innovative and unparalleled program for training Christians in relational evangelism. Adapt it to fit the needs of your church!

Curriculum Kit: 0-310-25785-9 (Includes all components)
Participant's Guide: 0-310-25787-5
Leader's Guide: 0-310-25786-7
DVD: 0-310-25788-3
Youth Curriculum: 0-310-23769-6

Also Available:

*Becoming a Contagious Christian:* 0-310-21008-9
*Becoming a Contagious Christian Spanish Edition:* 0-8297-3857-6